6.95

D1125884

SOCIETY FOR OLD TESTAMENT STUDY

MONOGRAPH SERIES

GENERAL EDITOR
J. A. EMERTON

1

THE HEAVENLY COUNSELLOR IN
ISAIAH xl 13–14

A STUDY OF THE SOURCES OF THE
THEOLOGY OF DEUTERO-ISAIAH

THE
HEAVENLY COUNSELLOR IN
ISAIAH xl 13-14

A STUDY OF
THE SOURCES OF THE THEOLOGY
OF DEUTERO-ISAIAH

R. N. WHYBRAY

*Reader in Theology in the
University of Hull*

CAMBRIDGE
AT THE UNIVERSITY PRESS
1971

Published by the Syndics of the Cambridge University Press
Bentley House, 200 Euston Road, London N.W.1
American Branch: 32 East 57th Street, New York, N.Y.10022

© Cambridge University Press 1971

Library of Congress Catalogue Card Number: 77–132286

ISBN: 0 521 08044 4

Printed in Great Britain
at the University Printing House, Cambridge
(Brooke Crutchley, University Printer)

CONTENTS

ACKNOWLEDGEMENTS

I desire to express my thanks to a number of persons who have read the typescript of this monograph at various stages of its preparation and offered both encouragement and criticism from which it has benefited: to Professors P. R. Ackroyd of King's College, London and James Barr of Manchester University; to my former colleague Mrs Mary Tanner; and in particular to Mr W. G. Lambert of Birmingham University, who has patiently criticized my use of Babylonian material and drawn my attention to many points and publications of which otherwise I should have been unaware. I also wish to thank Professor J. A. Emerton of Cambridge University, not only for a number of suggestions, but in particular for according my work the honour of inclusion in the Monograph Series of the Society for Old Testament Study.

ABBREVIATIONS

ANET	*Ancient Near Eastern Texts Relating to the Old Testament*, ed. J. B. Pritchard, Princeton, 1950; 2nd edn 1955
ASTI	*Annual of the Swedish Theological Institute in Jerusalem*
ATD	Das Alte Testament Deutsch, ed. A. Weiser
BDB	*A Hebrew and English Lexicon of the Old Testament*, ed. F. Brown, S. R. Driver and C. A. Briggs, Oxford, 1907
BWANT	Beiträge zur Wissenschaft vom Alten und Neuen Testament
BZAW	Beihefte zur *Zeitschrift für die Alttestamentliche Wissenschaft*
CBQ	*Catholic Biblical Quarterly*
G.-K.	*Gesenius' Hebrew Grammar*, ed. E. Kautzsch, translated by A. E. Cowley, Oxford, 1910
HAT	Handbuch zum Alten Testament, ed. O. Eissfeldt
HSAT	Die Heilige Schrift des Alten Testaments, ed. E. Kautzsch
HUCA	*Hebrew Union College Annual*
JAOS	*Journal of the American Oriental Society*
JBL	*Journal of Biblical Literature*
JNES	*Journal of Near Eastern Studies*
JSS	*Journal of Semitic Studies*
JTS	*Journal of Theological Studies*
KAT	Kommentar zum Alten Testament, Leipzig
KHAT	Kurzer Hand-Commentar zum Alten Testament, ed. K. Marti
OTL	Old Testament Library
RB	*Revue Biblique*
RSV	The Revised Standard Version
SBT	Studies in Biblical Theology

VT	*Vetus Testamentum*
VT Suppl.	Supplements to *Vetus Testamentum*
WMANT	Wissenschaftliche Monographien zum Alten und Neuen Testament
ZA	*Zeitschrift für Assyriologie*
ZAW	*Zeitschrift für die Alttestamentliche Wissenschaft*
ZDMG	*Zeitschrift der Deutschen Morgenländischen Gesellschaft*

INTRODUCTION[1]

One of the most rewarding of recent approaches to the study of Deutero-Isaiah has been the attempt to understand his teaching against the background of his ministry to the second generation of Jewish exiles in Babylonia.[2] Two factors have here to be taken into account: the nature of the Israelite religious tradition which the exiles had inherited from the past, and the actual circumstances of their life in Babylonia, where they were subject to the cultural and religious pressures of their environment. Each of these factors may be expected to have exercised some influence on the teaching of Deutero-Isaiah. It is in order to explore the relationship between the two that this study of one short passage has been undertaken. This passage, which has long been the subject of vigorous controversy, admirably raises the question of the sources of Deutero-Isaiah's theology, and it is hoped that a detailed study of it, employing as far as possible all the techniques of modern critical investigation, may shed some light on the interpretation of Deutero-Isaiah as a whole.

מִי־תִכֵּן אֶת־רוּחַ יְהוָה   וְאִישׁ עֲצָתוֹ יוֹדִיעֶנּוּ
אֶת־מִי נוֹעַץ וַיְבִינֵהוּ   וַיְלַמְּדֵהוּ בְּאֹרַח מִשְׁפָּט
וַיְלַמְּדֵהוּ דַעַת   וְדֶרֶךְ תְּבוּנוֹת יוֹדִיעֶנּוּ

13a   Who has directed the Spirit of the Lord,
 b   or as his counsellor has instructed him?
14a   Whom did he consult for his enlightenment,
 b   and who taught him the path of justice,
 c   and taught him knowledge,
 d   and showed him the way of understanding?[3]

---

[1] I am indebted to my colleague Mr P. J. Thompson for a remark about the possibility of a reference to wisdom in Isa. xl 13–14, which led me to undertake this investigation.

[2] An example is H.-E. von Waldow's 'Anlaß und Hintergrund der Verkündigung des Deuterojesaja' (unpublished dissertation), Bonn, 1953. A more recent summary of von Waldow's views is to be found in his 'The Message of Deutero-Isaiah', *Interpretation* 22 (1968), pp. 259–87.

[3] RSV translation.

A feature of Deutero-Isaiah's style which causes the greatest difficulties for his interpreters is his unusually frequent use of the question as a technique of argument.[1] This literary device is by no means peculiar to him: it is found in the Old Testament almost wherever rational argument occurs. It is used in a variety of ways, but in most cases the context leaves no room for doubt about its function. These functions have to some extent been classified in the lexica. But in the case of Deutero-Isaiah there are special difficulties. Often the nature of the context is itself a matter for debate. Whether these chapters are, as some have claimed,[2] a single composition with a continuity of thought, or, as most scholars maintain, a collection of short pieces, there is no general agreement about their internal divisions. Uncertainty about the structure of the thought frequently leads to uncertainty about the precise function of the questions.

The situation is particularly difficult in the case of the many questions beginning with, or involving, the particle 'who?' (מי). The answer expected may be positive or negative; and there is often a range of possibilities concerning the person or persons, thing or things referred to.

Ch. xl 13 f. is one of the passages concerning which there is wide disagreement. Most, though not all, commentators hold that the answers expected to these questions are negative; but even so there remain several possibilities concerning the identity of the person or persons whose role of adviser to Yahweh is thus implicitly denied. The reference may be to man: that is, no man could or did do these things. The point would then be that Yahweh is infinitely superior to man in his wisdom and knowledge. But it is also possible to interpret the

---

[1] Owing to this prophet's predilection for compound questions which may be taken either as single questions or as groups of separate questions, the exact number is difficult to compute. But in the 333 verses commonly attributed to Deutero-Isaiah there are certainly not less than 72, and perhaps as many as 85. The interrogative particle מי occurs 33 times (35, if two probable emendations are allowed).

[2] E.g. K. Budde, *Das Buch Jesaia Kap 40–66* (HSAT), 3rd edn 1909; more recently L. G. Rignell, *A Study of Isaiah Ch. 40–55*, Lund, 1956.

passage as referring to other gods or heavenly beings: as an assertion that Yahweh is superior to or independent of them. If this is the true meaning, the reference might be to a member or members of the Babylonian pantheon, or to an Israelite 'heavenly council' over which Yahweh is held to preside, such as is referred to in some of the Psalms and other passages in the Old Testament – a concept which probably has affinities with the assembly of the gods depicted in the Ugaritic literature. Again, the reference might be to some personified attribute of Yahweh such as wisdom: this view might appear to receive support from some other Old Testament texts such as Job xxviii, together with the fact that Yahweh's wisdom (דעת and תבונות) is here specifically mentioned. Finally it has been suggested[1] that the answer expected is positive: Deutero-Isaiah is declaring that it is the god El, mentioned a little later in verse 18, who advised and instructed Yahweh, so appearing to support a polytheistic view, but only in order to turn the tables in other passages where he declares that El and Yahweh are identical.[2]

The problem is one which is not without importance for the interpretation of the thought of Deutero-Isaiah as a whole. What is sometimes referred to as his 'doctrine of God' was not constructed in a vacuum, but, like the other aspects of his teaching, forms part of a reasoned apologetic whose aim was to convince his fellow exiles of the reasonableness of his central proclamation of imminent deliverance; and it can only be fully understood if we have a clear picture of the false beliefs which were under attack. It will be argued that these verses are to be understood against the background of a concept of an assembly of heavenly beings which was familiar to the Jews as part of their own religious traditions, but which the Jewish exiles in Babylonia had now encountered in a specifically Babylonian, polytheistic form which some of them found attractive, but which was incompatible with the Israelite understanding of God and threatened to hinder their acceptance of other aspects of Deutero-Isaiah's message.

[1] By P. A. H. de Boer, 'The Counsellor', *VT* Suppl. 3 (1955), p. 47.
[2] xliii 12; xlv 22.

CHAPTER I

THE CONTEXT

First it is necessary to examine the context of thought in which these verses are set. Many of the older scholars[1] regarded verses 12–31 as a literary unit, whether independent or not, mainly on the basis of their contents and style: the prophet here reasons with his audience, seeking to convince them of Yahweh's claim to total sovereignty. The use of the argument from creation and of the question form throughout the passage clearly distinguishes verses 12–31 both from what precedes and from what follows. Others[2] made a division between verse 26 and verse 27, recognising that the specific address to Jacob/Israel and the complaint about God's apparent injustice in verse 27 mark the beginning of a new section.

Within verses 12–26 (or 12–31) the older commentators generally recognised shorter sections, each presenting a particular aspect of the prophet's argument. But it was not until the techniques of form criticism were applied to Deutero-Isaiah that the possibility was envisaged that these shorter sections might in fact have originally been independent units.

Gressmann, the first to apply form critical methods, did not reach this conclusion because the hymnic themes and language which he identified here led him to classify the whole of verses 12–26 as a Hymn linked with a word of consolation (*Trostwort*, verses 27–31) to form a single composition.[3] It was Köhler, with a more precise understanding of individual forms, who narrowed the context, classifying verses 12–16 as a

---

[1] E.g. T. K. Cheyne, *The Prophecies of Isaiah*, 4th edn, 1886; K. Marti, *Das Buch Jesaja* (KHAT), 1900.

[2] E.g. P. Volz, *Jesaia II* (KAT), 1932; recently C. R. North, *The Second Isaiah*, Oxford, 1964.

[3] H. Gressmann, 'Die literarische Analyse Deuterojesajas' (*ZAW* **34** (1914), pp. 254–97), pp. 293 f. Gressmann recognised, however, that Deutero-Isaiah's 'Hymns' are only imitations of genuine cultic hymns, and that the hymnic form is here used to put forward an argument.

4

Disputation (*Streitgespräch*), a type of argument based on the forms of legal dispute in use in the administration of justice in the gate, a form which had already been used by some of the pre-exilic prophets.[1]

Further precision was attained by Begrich.[2] He recognised the necessity of distinguishing between the legal argument or judgement (*Gerichtsrede*) and the Disputation (*Disputationsrede*), a form of argument taken from daily life, which, although its general purpose is the same (to convince or persuade), has its own form consonant with its original *Sitz im Leben*. It is characteristic of the Disputation that it begins by pointing to common ground between the disputants, from which a conclusion favourable to the speaker's point of view and disproving that of his opponent is then drawn. Begrich recognised verses 12–17 as a Disputation, correcting on grounds of context, form and metre Köhler's view that the unit ends with verse 16.[3] Von Waldow[4] also regards these verses as a *Disputationswort*. The questions in verses 12–14 imply affirmations about Yahweh which constitute the common ground between the disputants, from which the prophet in verses 15–17 draws new conclusions. Like Begrich, von Waldow holds that the Disputation is derived from the forms of argument used in daily life, but maintains that Deutero-Isaiah in his Disputations also draws on other modes of speech. In these verses he adopts the style of the wisdom teacher.[5] Fohrer sees these verses as an imitation of the academic discussions (*Diskussionswort*) which took place in the wisdom schools.[6]

---

[1] L. Köhler, *Deuterojesaja (Jesaja 40–55) stilkritisch untersucht* (BZAW **37**), 1923, pp. 110–20.
[2] J. Begrich, *Studien zu Deuterojesaja* (BWANT **77 (25)**), 1938, pp. 41–6, reprinted as *Theologische Bücherei* **20**, Munich, 1963, pp. 48–53.
[3] *Theologische Bücherei*, p. 50 and note 168.
[4] 'Anlaß und Hintergrund', pp. 28–36, 135–47. For a discussion of von Waldow's views see C. Westermann, 'Sprache und Struktur der Prophetie Deuterojesajas' (*Forschung am alten Testament* (*Theologische Bücherei* **24**), Munich, 1964, pp. 127–32).
[5] 'The Message of Deutero-Isaiah', p. 269 n. 33.
[6] G. Fohrer, *Das Buch Jesaja*, vol. III (*Zürcher Bibelkommentare*), 1964, pp. 24–6.

Westermann[1] has attempted yet a further distinction. Within the *Disputationswort* he distinguishes two types: the true *Streitgespräch* or dispute between two opponents, in which the arguments of both sides are presented, even though one of them is given only in an abbreviated form; and the *Bestreitung* or single argument, in which only one side is given, in the form of a reasoned argument, while the other is left to be inferred. In Isa. xl 12–31 there are four examples of the *Disputationswort*, of which only the last (verses 27–31) is a true *Streitgespräch*, while the first three (verses 12–17, 18–24, 25–6) are to be classed as *Bestreitung*. Westermann thus agrees with some older scholars that verses 27–31 are to be distinguished from the previous verses, and provides a new explanation for this view; yet at the same time he holds to the view that the whole section (verses 12–31) really forms a single unit: the prophet has himself combined three examples of one type of disputation with one of another, and has bound them together as parts of a sustained argument. This, he maintains, is proved by verse 27: in this verse Jacob/Israel makes *two* complaints against God – that he cannot help, and that he will not. Only the second of these complaints is answered in the verses which follow (28–31); the first, already implicit in the three previous sections, has already received a triple answer there. Thus verse 27 looks both forwards and backwards, binding together the whole of verses 12–31 into a single unit.

Westermann also makes a further point. Deutero-Isaiah, in combining the form of the Disputation, originally taken from secular life, with that of the Psalm of Praise (*Lobpsalm*), which originally belonged to the cult, has created a new tool for persuading his audience to recognise their proper function as a cultic community devoted to the praise of God, and so a new kind of hortatory style, comparable in some ways to that of Deuteronomy.

Form-critical methods have thus confirmed the opinion of

[1] 'Sprache und Struktur der Prophetie Deuterojesajas', pp. 124–34.

some earlier critics that verses 12–17, whether they form part of a wider argument or not, constitute in some sense an argument which can stand by itself. Westermann has in addition confirmed the older view that they are to be regarded as the first of four such arguments which together make up a larger section. The form critics have also drawn attention to the fact that the style is composite, drawing upon cultic, and possibly wisdom, themes and language in order to reinforce the argument.

Verses 13 f. must therefore, it would seem, be interpreted within the context of verses 12–17, and possibly also within the wider context of verses 12–31. At first sight the wider of these two contexts would seem to provide comparative material which ought to throw light on the meaning of the questions with which we are concerned, since these questions now belong, if Westermann is right, to a series, of which other examples are found in verses 12, 18, 25 and 26. All these questions are similar to the extent that they are all posed in order to elicit a reply which confesses Yahweh's incomparability;[1] but it does not follow that the actual mechanism of the question is the same in each case; indeed, the fact that even within this short passage the prophet also uses the question technique in quite a different way (verses 21, 27, 28) may well increase our doubt on this point.[2] Apart from the use of questions, the prophet uses a wide variety of arguments: creation language in verse 12, straightforward assertions of human insignificance in verses 15, 17, 22–4; a mocking contrast between Yahweh and the idols in verses 19, 20; hymnic style in verse 22; a reference to Yahweh's power over the stars in verse 26; a reproach to

[1] On ways of expressing the incomparability of Yahweh see C. J. Labuschagne, *The Incomparability of Yahweh in the Old Testament (Pretoria Oriental Series* 5), Leiden, 1966, especially pp. 27 f.

[2] Begrich (*Studien zu Deuterojesaja*, p. 49 and notes 165, 166) referred to the predilection for the use of the question as the starting-point of the Disputation, but pointed out that its function is not always the same in each case. He held that in verses 12–14 the questions state the common ground between the disputants, whereas in verses 18, 25 and 27 they pose the question at issue between them.

Jacob/Israel for lack of faith in verse 27; a comforting description of Yahweh as helper of the weak in verses 28–31. Manifestly we cannot say of a prophet who had such a wide command of thought and language that whenever he uses a particular kind of question he must use it for the same purpose. Consequently the context provided by verses 12–31 sheds no light on our problem; and this is, for the same reason, equally true of the even wider context of chapters 40–55.

It is unfortunately no less true even of the narrower context of verses 12–17. The fact that verses 12–14 consist entirely of questions beginning with 'Who?', 'Whom?' or 'With whom?' has led some scholars[1] to maintain that the answer to all these questions is the same: 'no man'. Westermann[2] argues that there is an *a fortiori* argument here: if the answer to the questions in verse 12, e.g. 'Who has measured the waters in the hollow of his hand?', is that man is unable to do this, then the questions in verses 13 f. mean 'How much less, then, could man have directed the Spirit of Yahweh?'

But this interpretation is by no means certain. The meaning of verse 12 itself is in dispute. The question asked here has the same form as some of the questions put to Job by God in Job xxxviii–xxxix;[3] but the answer to those questions need not be 'no man'; it may be 'not you, Job', or 'I, Yahweh'. A number of commentators interpret Isa. xl 12 similarly, maintaining that the answer expected is either 'Yahweh'[4] or 'no one but Yahweh'.[5] The question would then be intended to rule out not only man, but all other beings human and

[1] E.g. Volz, *Jesaia II* (KAT); B. Couroyer, 'Isaïe, XL, 12', *RB* **73** (1966), pp. 186–96; C. Westermann, *Das Buch Jesaja Kapitel 40–66* (ATD), 1966; J. L. McKenzie, *Second Isaiah* (Anchor Bible), 1968.

[2] Commentary, *ad loc.*

[3] Especially xxxviii 5, 8, 25; xxxix 5.

[4] So, e.g., J. Skinner, *Isaiah Chapters XL–LXVI* (Cambridge Bible), 2nd edn 1917; B. Duhm, *Das Buch Jesaia* (Göttinger Handkommentar), 4th edn 1922; Fohrer; North.

[5] So, e.g., Cheyne and Marti. Labuschagne (*The Incomparability of Yahweh*, pp. 19, 27) understands all the questions in verses 12–14 as expecting the answer 'no one, except Yahweh', but it is difficult to see how this can be true of the questions in verses 13, 14.

divine. Either of these interpretations is possible, and both find parallels in other passages in the Old Testament. In Deutero-Isaiah itself some questions of this type[1] are specifically given the positive answer, 'I, Yahweh' and 'Was it not I, Yahweh?', although in another passage[2] the answer is obviously negative.[3] With regard to the possibility that the answer is intended to exclude divine beings as well as or instead of men, we may compare Deut. iii 24, 'What god is there in heaven or on earth who can do such works and mighty acts as thine?'.

Even if we allow the possibility that the questions in Isa. xl 12 require the answer 'no man', it is by no means certain that this is also true of verses 13 f. The *a fortiori* argument discovered here by Westermann turns out on examination to be nothing of the kind. To proceed from the question whether man can create the world to ask whether human skill was behind the creator to guide him adds nothing to the force of the argument, and is not directly suggested by it. The questions are parallel, not identical and not consecutive. We are therefore forced to conclude that they may be different types of question, and consequently we are unable to use the immediate any more than the general context to determine the sense of verses 13 f.

[1] xli 4, 'Who has performed and done this?'; xlii 24, 'Who gave up Jacob to the spoiler?'.

[2] xlviii 14: 'Who among them has declared these things?'.

[3] Outside Deutero-Isaiah we may also compare, e.g. Exod. iv 11: 'Who has made man's mouth?... Is it not I, Yahweh?'.

CHAPTER II

DETAILED INTERPRETATION

We turn to an examination of the literal meaning of the passage.[1]

It is clear that the hypothetical situation here envisaged, only to be denied, is one in which there exists some person or being who gave Yahweh the benefit of his wisdom and experience. This is emphasised by the piling up of verbs meaning 'to teach' with Yahweh as object: הוֹדִיעַ twice; הֵבִין and לִמַּד once each. The scene is one in which Yahweh is represented as taking advice. In verse 13b, which should probably be rendered[2] 'and (who) was his counsellor who instructed him?', אִישׁ עֵצָה clearly has a meaning virtually identical with that of יוֹעֵץ, 'counsellor'.[3] It should here be noted that the use of the word אִישׁ does not restrict the reference to human beings: even Yahweh, in a metaphor, can be called אִישׁ מִלְחָמָה (Exod. xv 3).

Verse 13a must be interpreted in the light of 13b, with which it is parallel. The former has long been a source of controversy. RSV translates it 'Who has directed the Spirit of the Lord?'; but the meaning of the verb תִּכֵּן is disputed, and it is necessary to define more closely what is meant here by the רוּחַ of Yahweh.

LXX has τίς ἔγνω νοῦν κυρίου, 'Who has understood the mind of the Lord?'. There is reason to believe that this is the true sense. רוּחַ here refers to the 'mind' of Yahweh, including both his purpose and his practical intelligence and ability. When used of human attributes it frequently means 'temper, mood, disposition'; but in at least two passages it clearly

---

[1] The consensus of the commentators that the words וילמדהו דעת in verse 14c, which appear to have no equivalent in LXX, are a later repetitive insertion into the text is here assumed to be correct.

[2] With Marti, Duhm, Fohrer, North, Westermann et al.

[3] See further below, pp. 27–9.

10

refers to the human mind or thoughts. In Ezek. xx 32 it is in the רוּחַ that a thought or plan is formed. 1 Chron. xxviii 12 similarly refers to the plan which David 'had in mind' (הָיָה בָרוּחַ עִמּוֹ) for the building of the Temple. It has been maintained by some scholars[1] that בָּרוּחַ here means 'through the Spirit (of God)', on the grounds that רוּחַ is never used elsewhere by the Chronicler with reference to men. This is true; but it is equally true that the Chronicler never elsewhere uses the phrase הָרוּחַ absolutely of God![2] In fact, the use of הָרוּחַ absolutely of God is very rare in the Old Testament. In Ezekiel רוּחַ occurs frequently by itself, though without the article; but in every case it can be translated 'wind' or 'breath': its function is to set the prophet on his feet[3] or to lift him up and transport him to another place,[4] and it is to be identified with the 'stormy wind' of i 4. In Hos. ix 7 the phrase אִישׁ הָרוּחַ is parallel with 'prophet'; but here רוּחַ is used adjectivally, the article qualifying the whole phrase: 'spirit-filled man'. In Num. xxvii 18; Isa. xxxii 15 there is no article; in Isa. lvii 16, where also there is no article, רוּחַ is parallel with 'breath of life'. The only passage which might be compared with the supposed usage in 1 Chron. xxviii 12 is Num. xi 26, where the Spirit is some kind of measurable substance which rests on Moses and is then shared out between him and the elders.

The evidence is thus very slender indeed for the theory that in 1 Chron. xxviii 12 הָרוּחַ refers to divine inspiration. The phrase הָיָה עִמּוֹ by itself means 'it was his intention';[5] the addition of בָּרוּחַ strengthens the statement: 'in his mind'.[6] We might expect the addition of a suffix, i.e. בְּרוּחוֹ;

---

[1] E.g. W. Rudolph, *Chronikbücher* (HAT), 1955; J. M. Myers, *I Chronicles* (Anchor Bible), 1965.

[2] In 1 Chron. xii 19 there is no article, and the case is quite different: 'a spirit' clothes itself with Amasai – a reflection of an old formula which we find in earlier literature in the Books of Judges and Samuel.

[3] ii 2; iii 24.

[4] iii 12, 14; viii 3; xi 1, 24; xliii 5.

[5] 1 Kings xi 11; Job x 13; cf. Job xxiii 14.

[6] It is conceivable that the two phrases may originally have been alternative readings which have been preserved side by side. See S. Talmon, 'Double

but there are other instances of the omission of the suffix in similar circumstances.[1]

There are also a number of passages where רוּחַ is used in connection with God[2] and may have the sense of 'mind, intelligence'. In Isa. xxx 1 God condemns those who have 'made a plan (עֵצָה), but it is not from me (מִנִּי); entered into an alliance, but it is not [sic] my Spirit (רוּחִי)'. Here, although the reference could be to divine inspiration, the context suggests that the point is rather that the plans are doomed to failure (verses 3–5) because they proceed from the defective intelligence of (rebellious) children (verse 1) rather than from the superior practical intelligence of God. Similarly in Exod. xxxi 3; xxxv 31, where it is said that Bezalel was filled with רוּחַ אֱלֹהִים, this phrase is followed by a list of words preceded by the *beth essentiae*,[3] indicating that in this case רוּחַ is to be defined in terms of דַּעַת, תְּבוּנָה, חָכְמָה, etc., that is as practical intelligence.[4] On the other hand, when this author wishes to refer to divine inspiration he uses a different phrase, נָתַן בְּלִבּוֹ (xxxv 34). Finally in Ps. cxliii 10 ('Teach me to do thy will,...let thy good Spirit lead me'), the use of the word 'teach' may suggest the meaning 'mind, intelligence' for רוּחַ.

These considerations are not, perhaps, conclusive; but they at least leave open the possibility that in Isa. xl 13a also the רוּחַ of Yahweh should be translated 'mind' in the sense of practical intelligence; and this meaning accords better with

Readings in the Massoretic Text', *Textus* **1** (1960), pp. 144–84; 'Synonymous Readings in the Textual Tradition of the Old Testament', *Scripta Hierosolymitana* **8** (1961), pp. 335–83. This possibility does not affect the present argument.

1 E.g. with לֵב: 2 Sam. xviii 3; Isa. xlii 25; xlvi 8.

2 Though never absolutely and with the article as has been alleged in the case of 1 Chron. xxviii 12.

3 On this usage see G.-K. 119 i, where, however, this passage is not cited.

4 It is, however, possible that רוּחַ אֱלֹהִים means 'excellent רוּחַ' and is thus a human and not a divine attribute. See D. Winton Thomas, 'A Consideration of Some Unusual Ways of Expressing the Superlative in Hebrew', *VT* **3** (1953), pp. 209–24; 'Some Further Remarks on Unusual Ways of Expressing the Superlative in Hebrew', *VT* **18** (1968), pp. 120–4.

the context, which speaks of intellectual ability (יוֹדִיעֶנּוּ in the parallel clause) than any other.[1]

The meaning of תִּכֵּן is also disputed. Here again LXX's ἔγνω is not followed by modern translations; but it has been supported by some modern discussion.

According to Dhorme[2] the basic meaning of the root תכן is 'gauge', i.e. 'estimate (the size, weight, shape, proportion etc. of) a thing by comparing it with a standard'. According to Driver, however,[3] it is 'adjust (to standard), set right'; and such translations as 'estimate', 'mete out' and the like are unjustified. Since these sets of meanings are by no means opposites, but refer to actions which frequently go hand in hand, it is not surprising that in a number of cases where the verb תכן occurs in the Old Testament either sense seems to fit the context equally well.

Thus in Job xxviii 25, מַיִם תִּכֵּן בְּמִדָּה (parallel to 'giving to the wind its weight') could mean either 'adjusted (the limits of) the waters by measure' (Driver) or 'gauge(d) the waters with a measure' (Dhorme–Knight).[4] In 2 Kings xii 12 הַכֶּסֶף הַמְתֻכָּן may mean 'silver adjusted (to standard)'[5] rather than 'silver which was counted out, estimated'. In Isa. xl 12 (שָׁמַיִם בַּזֶּרֶת תִּכֵּן) there is effectively little difference between 'has adjusted the heavens with a span' (Driver) and 'measured with a span', since the one action implies the other.

---

[1] It may be worth noting that it is used several times in the Old Testament from about the time of the exile in connection with *building activity*: apart from the example of Bezalel, it was the *spirit* of the people which was stirred by God to build the Temple after the return (Ezra i 5) and again when the work was resumed under Zerubbabel (Hag. i 14); and it was the *spirit* of Cyrus which was stirred by God to permit the Jews to return to Palestine with the specific intention that they should build the Temple (2 Chron. xxxvi 22 f.). It may be that this association of רוּחַ with positive practical activity is significant for the interpretation of Isa. xl 13 also.

[2] E. Dhorme, *Le Livre de Job* (*Études Bibliques*), Paris, 1926 (English translation by Harold Knight, *A Commentary on the Book of Job*, London, 1967) on Job xxviii 25. Cf. also G. Fohrer, *Das Buch Hiob* (KAT), 1963, *ad loc.*

[3] G. R. Driver, 'Hebrew Notes', *VT* **1** (1951), pp. 242 f.

[4] 'Jauger les eaux avec une mesure' in the French.

[5] On the process involved here see O. Eissfeldt, 'Eine Einschmelzstelle am Tempel zu Jerusalem', *Forschungen und Fortschritte* **13** (1937), pp. 163–4 (= *Kleine Schriften* **2**, pp. 107–9).

In the case of the cognate nouns, the precise meaning of which is in any case not clear in every instance, it is again difficult to distinguish between the senses of 'adjustment' and 'estimating, meting out': תֹּכֶן, 'standard or required quantity', Exod. v 18; Ezek. xlv 11; מַתְכֹּנֶת, 'standard of measurement', Ezek. xlv 11; possibly 'composition' (i.e. according to the required or fixed standard recipe) of the holy oil, Exod. xxx 32; תָּכְנִית, 'pattern' or 'standard prescribed form' of the Temple, Ezek. xliii 10; possibly the 'perfection', i.e. conformity to the true norm of beauty, of a signet ring, Ezek. xxviii 12.

In some cases, however, one or other of the proposed meanings is clearly more appropriate. Thus in Ezek. xviii 25, 29; xxxiii 17–20, where it is said of God that לֹא יִתָּכֵן דֶּרֶךְ אֲדֹנָי, and where God turns the tables and makes the same accusation against his accusers, the context makes it clear that the phrase means 'Yahweh's behaviour is not equitable'. Here Driver's sense of 'not adjusted (to ordinary standards)' appears certain. This is also true of the much discussed Ps. lxxv 4, where God is represented as giving an assurance that when the earth totters, he will not permit it to collapse: אָנֹכִי תִכַּנְתִּי עַמּוּדֶיהָ. Although this might be understood as meaning that he has gauged or correctly estimated the pillars which support the earth, making each the standard for the others,[1] it is more natural to take it as meaning that he adjusts or sets them right.

On the other hand there are four passages where the meaning 'gauge, estimate' seems to be the only possible one. In Prov. xvi 2 the verb is used in the Qal, and Yahweh is said to be תֹּכֵן רוּחוֹת; in Prov. xxi 2; xxiv 12 he is תֹּכֵן לִבּוֹת; and in I Sam. ii 3, where the Niphal is used, it is said of God that לוֹ נִתְכְּנוּ עֲלִלוֹת.[2] In themselves these phrases might be interpreted in Driver's sense of 'adjust, set right'; God may undoubtedly be said to set man's heart or spirit right. But the

[1] So e.g. M. Dahood, *Psalms II (51–100)* (Anchor Bible), 1968, *ad loc.*

[2] Reading לוֹ for לֹא with some MSS, Qere and Vulgate.

context in each case makes this sense most unlikely. In every case the point is God's ability to gauge or estimate correctly the state of man's heart rather than his putting it right. In Prov. xvi 2; xxi 2 a contrast is made between man's ignorance of his sin and God's perception of it; in Prov. xxiv 12; 1 Sam. ii 3 the point is the impossibility of hiding one's sin from the all-knowing God. In Prov. xxiv 12 it is stated that he who gauges the hearts *is* the one who understands (הוּא־יָבִין); and in 1 Sam. ii 3 the statement that men's deeds are gauged by Yahweh is parallel with a statement that he is a God of knowledge (אֵל דֵּעוֹת).

It would seem, therefore, that whether 'gauge, estimate' is the original meaning of the root or not, there are passages where this is the only meaning which makes sense, even though in other passages 'adjust, set right' is more appropriate.

In the four cases considered above the verb is in the Qal or Niphal; Isa. xl 13 has the Piel. There is, however, no reason why the Piel should not have a sense similar to that of the Qal, especially in view of the similarity between תִּכֵּן רוּחַ here and תֹּכֵן רוּחוֹת in Prov. xvi 2.[1]

In any case it is doubtful whether Driver's rendering 'Who has set right, directed the Spirit of Yahweh?' can be justified even on his own interpretation of the basic meaning of the root. To adjust and to direct, in the only sense which the latter word can bear here, are by no means the same thing. Driver appears to have jumped from the one to the other as

---

[1] It might be argued that תכן in Isa. xl 13 was intended to be read as Qal, but that the pointing was assimilated to the תִּכֵּן of the previous verse. This, however, would be purely speculative and unnecessary. That the prophet should use the verb in two somewhat different senses in consecutive verses need occasion no surprise. Whether paronomasia and other kinds of word-play are especially characteristic of Deutero-Isaiah or not, there can be no doubt that this prophet, like other Old Testament prophets, does make use of them on a number of occasions. See D. F. Payne, 'Old Testament Exegesis and the Problem of Ambiguity', *ASTI* 5 (1966/7), pp. 48–68; 'Characteristic Word-Play in "Second Isaiah"', *JSS* 12 (1967), pp. 207–29; P. R. Ackroyd, 'Meaning and Exegesis', *Words and Meanings, Essays Presented to D. W. Thomas*, Cambridge, 1968, pp. 1–14.

a result of an ambiguity in the meaning of the English word
'direct'. On his own argument, the choice must be between
'adjust (to a standard)' and 'gauge, estimate'. 'Who has
adjusted the Spirit of Yahweh?' makes little sense. On the
other hand, 'Who has gauged the mind of Yahweh?' is not
only an intelligible sentence, but is also extremely appropriate
to the context. The clauses which follow enquire whether
there is any being capable of giving instruction to Yahweh.
Such a being would necessarily possess an intelligence
superior to, or more mature than, that of Yahweh. To gauge
is to comprehend; and consequently the most natural interpretation of the whole clause is that of LXX: 'Who has
comprehended the mind of Yahweh?'[1]

We must next ask what kind of instruction and advice is
supposedly given to Yahweh here. It is described in verse 14*bd*:
וַיְלַמְּדֵהוּ בְּאֹרַח מִשְׁפָּט וְדֶרֶךְ תְּבוּנוֹת יוֹדִיעֶנּוּ. The two clauses are
exactly parallel in form. Both דֶרֶךְ and אֹרַח here mean 'the
proper way (of doing something)'. דֶרֶךְ is used in this sense
in the phrase 'the way of life' (e.g. Prov. vi 23), i.e. 'the
proper way of living (so as to obtain fullness of life)',[2] and
similarly with שָׁלוֹם (Isa. lix 8), חָכְמָה (Prov. iv 11), בִּינָה
(Prov. ix 6), הַשְׂכֵּל (Prov. xxi 16). In Jer. xxi 8 'the way of life
and the way of death' means, as the following verse shows,
'what you must do if you are to live, and what you must do
if you are to die'. אֹרַח is also used in exactly the same way
(Ps. xvi 11; Prov. ii 19; v 6; x 17).

It is also clear from other Old Testament passages that
this kind of 'way' can be taught. In 1 Sam. xii 23; Ps. xxv 8,
12; xxxii 8; Prov. iv 11 the phrase הוֹרָה בַּדֶרֶךְ or הוֹרָה בְדֶרֶךְ
occurs, with the person taught in the accusative. This phrase,
meaning 'teach (someone) the proper way (to do something)',

---

[1] There is thus no need to suppose, as did, e.g. Duhm and Skinner, that LXX's
ἔγνω is a translation of some other word such as הֵבִין.

[2] On this phrase see E. Schmitt, *Leben in den Weisheitsbüchern Job, Sprüche und
Jesus Sirach* (*Freiburger Theologische Studien* 66), Freiburg, 1954, pp. 95 f. On
דֶרֶךְ and אֹרַח see H. Duesberg and I. Fransen, *Les Scribes Inspirés* (2nd edn),
Maredsous, 1966, pp. 225–8.

is exactly equivalent to וַיְלַמְּדֵהוּ בְּאֹרַח מִשְׁפָּט, even to the idiomatic use of בְּ before 'way' rather than the use of a double accusative. We may therefore compare the phrases אֹרַח מִשְׁפָּט and דֶּרֶךְ תְּבוּנוֹת with דֶּרֶךְ חַיִּים, דֶּרֶךְ שָׁלוֹם etc., and conclude that the two phrases in Isa. xl 14 mean 'and taught him the proper way of doing (or achieving) תְּבוּנוֹת/מִשְׁפָּט'.

But what, in this context, is the meaning of מִשְׁפָּט and תְּבוּנוֹת? מִשְׁפָּט is a word with a very wide range of meanings, one of which is 'way, manner'. It might appear, therefore, in view of what has been said above concerning אֹרַח, that the phrase בְּאֹרַח מִשְׁפָּט is tautologous. But in fact there are instances in which the word מִשְׁפָּט is used in a more restricted sense. In Exod. xxvi 30; 1 Kings vi 38; Ezek. xlii 11 it is used in connection with building – of the Tabernacle, the Temple of Solomon, and the Temple of Ezekiel respectively. In all these passages it refers to the design or arrangement of the building, whether of the original plan according to which it is (to be) built, or of the completed building itself. A somewhat similar meaning is found in Isa. xxviii 26, where the operations of the farmer are said to be done according to divine instructions: he is instructed לַמִּשְׁפָּט. In these cases the word appears to refer to something done in the right way, according to the correct principles. It is very close to the wisdom vocabulary of חָכְמָה and its synonyms בִּינָה and תְּבוּנָה, which signify practical knowledge of what to do. It is also to be noted that the word had a special association with building and construction. It is therefore possible to translate אֹרַח מִשְׁפָּט by 'the way of achieving a proper order (in what one does)'.

That the reference here is to God's creative skill is confirmed by the parallel phrase דֶּרֶךְ תְּבוּנוֹת.[1] תְּבוּנָה connotes skilful craftsmanship,[2] and is, among other things, needed for the building of a house.[3] Further, in a number of passages[4]

---

[1] Plural of intensification (G.-K. 124 e).
[2] Exod. xxxi 3; xxxv 31; xxxvi 1; 1 Kings vii 14.　　　　[3] Prov. xxiv 3.
[4] Jer. x 12 = li 15; Job xii 13; xxvi 12 (the smiting of Rahab); Ps. cxxxvi 5; Prov. iii 19.

it is stated that it was through his possession of it that God created the world. It is also used in this connection in another passage in this very chapter: in xl 28 it is said of Yahweh the Creator that there is no limit to his תְּבוּנָה.

We therefore suggest that the content of the supposed knowledge taught to Yahweh in these verses is the practical knowledge required to create the world; and we translate them as follows:

> Who has understood the mind of Yahweh,
>> or who was his counsellor, who instructed him?
> Whom did he consult for his guidance,
>> and who taught him the way to achieve order,
> And showed him how to exercise creative skill?

CHAPTER III

LITERARY CHARACTERISTICS

Our next enquiry is into the background of the vocabulary and literary forms used in these verses. Four formal characteristics may be distinguished:

a. The verses consist of a series of questions, each beginning with or containing the word מִי, 'Who?'.

b. They contain a high proportion of words which are characteristic of, though not peculiar to, the wisdom literature: אֹרַח, תְּבוּנָה, עֵצָה (in its metaphorical sense).

c. Certain phrases suggest a political setting; that is, a political consultation between the king and his courtiers: אִישׁ עֲצָתוֹ, אֶת־מִי נוֹעָץ.

d. No less than three verbs are used which mean 'teach, instruct', with Yahweh as their object: הֵבִין, לִמֵּד, הוֹדִיעַ.

A. QUESTIONS

(1) *The question form.* As has already been pointed out, the use of questions is characteristic of the style of Deutero-Isaiah. It is also characteristic of the wisdom books of the Old Testament, especially Job and Ecclesiastes; but there is no reason to suppose Deutero-Isaiah to have been specifically influenced by wisdom circles in this respect. The question is used frequently throughout the Old Testament as a stylistic device wherever there is a discussion or argument between two or more persons. It is, for example, with a question that the serpent begins his persuasive speech to Eve (Gen. iii 1); with a question that Samuel begins his condemnation of Saul after the latter's failure to devote the Amalekite spoil (1 Sam. xv 14); and with a question that Elijah is instructed by God to confront Ahab after the murder of Naboth (1 Kings xxi 19). All these questions are rhetorical in that

they do not seek genuine information; examples could easily be multiplied. It is hardly too much to say that the rhetorical question is the principal device of Hebrew rhetoric and oratory. It is especially frequent in the wisdom books because it is there that we find the most sustained arguments and discussions. These books make use of a rich variety of types of question for widely differing purposes, both – especially in Job – in the cut and thrust of argument between opponents and – in Proverbs and Ecclesiastes – in the calmer didactic atmosphere of the wisdom instruction. But the use of questions is not sufficient by itself to establish a literary genre.[1]

(2) *Series of questions.* These verses do not merely use the question form: they consist entirely of questions, and if we include verse 12 also, we have here a fairly lengthy series. This is also a stylistic device found frequently in the Old Testament. A single speaker seeks to overwhelm his adversary by bombarding him with a string of unanswerable questions. The best known example of this is the long series of questions which God puts to Job in Job xxxviii–xxxix. But, like the use of the question technique in general, this technique also is not confined to the wisdom literature. It is found also in narrative works. The best example there may be defined as a political, or, more specifically, a diplomatic interchange: that between the messengers of Hezekiah and the Assyrian Rabshakeh in 2 Kings xviii 19–36. This passage contains two extended speeches by the Rabshakeh (verses 19–25, 28–35), separated by a brief argument with the messengers of the king in verses 26 f. The first speech consists almost entirely of questions (five in seven verses!); the second begins with an

---

[1] There is as yet no comprehensive study of the use of the question form in the Old Testament. See, however, E. König, *Stilistik, Rhetorik, Poetik im Bezug auf die biblische Literatur*, Leipzig, 1900, especially pp. 150, 228 f. The role of certain types of question in specific *Gattungen* is, however, receiving increasing attention: e.g. H.-J. Boecker, *Redeformen des Rechtslebens im Alten Testament*, Neukirchen, 1964 (on legal usage); Labuschagne, *The Incomparability of Yahweh in the O.T.* (on expressions of incomparability); G. W. Coats, *Rebellion in the Wilderness*, Nashville, 1968 (on the 'murmuring motif').

exhortation (verses 28*b*–32), but ends with three verses which consist entirely of questions. The questions are very varied: the Rabshakeh sees, for example, no inconsistency in arguing on the one hand that Yahweh is powerless (verses 22, 33–5) and on the other that it is at his bidding that the Assyrian king has invaded Judah (verse 25). For the Jewish reader there is a dramatic irony in some of the questions; but seen as an example of political argument (and there is no reason to suppose that it is not based on the actual rhetorical style of the day), the speech is intended to overwhelm the speaker's opponents by means of unanswerable, rhetorical questions. So powerful was this device considered to be that in the final speech the climax consists entirely of such questions: no further positive assertions are deemed to be necessary to drive home the point.

An analysis of the types of question used in this passage and a comparison of them with the types of question used in Job xxxviii–xxxix would show that every type used by the Rabshakeh is also found in Job. The style is that of the formal argument, whether political or academic.

(3) *Questions beginning with or containing* מי. This type of question is one of those most frequently employed in argument.[1] Apart from its primary function of enquiring about the identity of a person or group of persons, it is employed in a variety of rhetorical functions, in which it partially or even totally loses its proper interrogative force. This variety of usage is such that in some cases the point is not always clear.

Like other rhetorical questions in Hebrew and other languages, this type of question is frequently used to give emphasis to an affirmation (or negation) and so to persuade or force an opponent into acceptance. In many cases the affirmation is made explicit in the words which follow, e.g. Exod. iv 11, 'Who made man's mouth...? Is it not I,

---

[1] There are examples in almost every book of the Old Testament. Deutero-Isaiah has 33 examples and the relatively brief speech of the Rabshakeh in 2 Kings xviii two. Job xxxviii–xxxix has the highest concentration.

Yahweh?'. But in many more the affirmation is merely implied. It is here that ambiguity may arise concerning the person or persons to whom reference is made. There are also, as the examples below will illustrate, other more idiomatic types in which the interrogative function has been entirely lost. Further, some emotion such as contempt, surprise, doubt or desire is frequently present, and this also has to be inferred.

In nominal clauses the question may imply the insignificance of the person referred to, as in the self-depreciatory 'Who am I!' (e.g. Exod. iii 11; 1 Sam. xviii 18; 2 Sam. vii 18) and the contemptuous 'Who is X?' (e.g. Exod. v 2; Judg. ix 28, 38; 1 Sam. xvii 26). More frequently it calls for a negative answer, though often with a positive implication: followed by the comparative כְּ ('Who is like X?') it implies the uniqueness or incomparability of someone or something (e.g. Exod. xv 11, 'O Yahweh, who is like thee?'; 1 Sam. xxvi 15; Ps. xxxv 10; Jer. xlix 19). Similarly, followed by a noun and the relative אֲשֶׁר (e.g. Deut. iv 7, 'What people is there who...?'; cf. Deut. iii 24; iv 8; v 26), or in expressions like 'Who is God but...?' (2 Sam. xxii 32; cf. Isa. xlii 19), uniqueness is implied.[1] In these cases also the answer expected is a negative one, but the effect is that of a positive statement; the intention, moreover, is not argument but a confession of faith. Elsewhere, however, מִי in a nominal sentence is used as a device for dramatising a statement about to be made, as in the series of questions in Prov. xxiii 29 f. ('Who has woe?', etc., answered in the following verse, 'Those who tarry long over wine') or Isa. lxiii 1 ('Who is this that comes from Edom?...It is I.').

A similar variety of usage is found in מִי followed by the

---

[1] For a full discussion see Labuschagne, *The Incomparability of Yahweh*. The view of B. Hartmann ('Es gibt keinen Gott ausser Jahwe: zur generellen Verneinung im Hebräischen', *ZDMG* **110** (NF **35**) (1961), pp. 229–35) that in some cases מִי is not an interrogative, but is derived from a proto-Semitic *mâ* = 'not' (rejected by Labuschagne, pp. 12–14) does not seem to have been generally accepted.

imperfect. Here 'Who can...?' frequently implies extreme difficulty or impossibility, often with a further implication of human weakness or limitation (e.g. Gen. xlix 9; 1 Sam. ii 25; Job xiv 4). Yet in other cases it expresses arrogance, as in Ps. lxiv 6, 'Who can see us?'; Jer. xxi 13, 'Who shall come down against us?'. 'Who would listen to you?' (1 Sam. xxx 24) is contemptuous. But the construction can also be used to express a wish, e.g. 2 Sam. xv 4, 'Who will make me judge in the land?', which has the force of 'O that I were...!' (cf. Num. xi 4). The verb used most frequently in this connection is מִי יִתֵּן: נָתַן has become a stereotyped expression which sometimes has only a very loose syntactical relationship with the rest of the sentence, e.g. Deut. v 29; Job xxiii 3.[1] With the participle, mainly in the expression מִי יוֹדֵעַ, there is a similar variety of meaning: this phrase may indicate a hopeful possibility (2 Sam. xii 22; Joel ii 14; Jonah iii 9; Esther iv 14), human ignorance (Ps. xc 11; Eccles. vi 12) or doubt (Eccles. ii 19; iii 21).

This extreme variety of usage with its consequent likelihood of ambiguity is also found when מִי is used with the perfect.[2] Most frequent is the implied negation, in which the answer expected is 'no-one'. We have already encountered an example of this in 2 Kings xviii 35: 'Who among the gods has delivered...?'. However, when God is the speaker, or when it is his activity which is referred to, it is often difficult to determine whether the answer should be 'no man' or '(I,) God'. This is true of the questions in Job xxxviii–xxxix and in Prov. xxx 4. But elsewhere the question is asked merely as a way of emphasising the statement which follows: 'Who killed Abimelech? Did not a woman...?' (2 Sam. xi 21); 'Who made man's mouth...? Is it not I, Yahweh?' (Exod. iv 11). In other cases the question form has become

---

[1] For further examples see Brockelmann, *Syntax*, 9.

[2] The ambiguities are due partly to the inevitably imperfect acquaintance of the modern reader with the idioms of an ancient language, but also partly to the transference of an originally oral idiom into a literary context. In oral usage the tone of voice would have made the meaning clear.

simply an idiomatic expression conveying an accusation: 'Who told you that you are naked?' (Gen. iii 11); 'Who made you a prince...over us?' (Exod. ii 14); 'Who has required of you this trampling of my courts?' (Isa. i 12). Similarly 'Who has heard...?' and 'Who has seen...?' (Isa. lxvi 8; Jer. xviii 13) are no more than expressions of astonishment.

The above list of usages could be greatly extended. In the majority of cases the context sufficiently indicates the function of the rhetorical question; but where it does not do so, ambiguity necessarily arises. An examination of the other cases (i.e. apart from xl 13 f.) where מִי is used with the perfect in Deutero-Isaiah will illustrate the variety of meaning and the occasional ambiguity of this construction.

In a number of passages the point of the question is a contrast between the power of Yahweh and the impotence of the other gods, and thus in a sense one may say that a double answer is implied: 'none (of the gods)', and 'Yahweh alone'. The answers are sometimes explicitly given and sometimes only implied; and in the latter case it is not always clear which of the two answers is to be regarded as primary.

The ambiguity of the questions in xl 12 has already been referred to.[1] In xli 2, 4 the two questions 'Who has stirred up one from the east...?' and 'Who has performed and done this...?' are answered positively in verse 4: 'I, Yahweh'. In xli 26, 'Who declared it from the beginning...?' is answered both negatively ('There was none who declared it', verse 26b) and positively (verse 27).[2] In xlii 24, to the question 'Who gave up Jacob to the spoiler...?' a positive

---

[1] Pp. 8 f., above.

[2] The first half of the verse (רִאשׁוֹן לְצִיּוֹן הִנֵּה הִנָּם) is unintelligible. The context suggests that it originally contained a statement by Yahweh giving a positive answer to the question. This view is common to the reconstructions of the text in many commentaries (Duhm, Marti, North, Köhler, Westermann, Fohrer, McKenzie) and also C. F. Whitley (*JSS* **2** (1957), pp. 327 f.) although their reconstructions differ in detail. G. R. Driver, however (*Alttestamentliche Studien* (*F. Nötscher Festschrift*), Bonn, 1950, pp. 46 f.), takes a different view.

answer is given: 'Was it not Yahweh...?', but there is also an implicit denial that it was the gods of the victorious Babylonians. In xliv 7*b*, where the unintelligible text should probably be restored to read something like 'Who has announced from of old things to come?',[1] there is again an implied negative answer pointing to the impotence of the other gods, but this is followed in verse 8 by a positive one: 'Have I not told you from of old...?'. In xlv 21 the questions 'Who told this long ago? Who declared it of old?' are addressed to the supporters of the other gods, whose silence implies an inability to give a positive answer on their behalf; but a positive answer from Yahweh follows: 'Was it not I, Yahweh?' In xlviii 14 the form of the question 'Who among them[2] has declared these things?' again requires a negative answer that the gods have been unable to do so, though the following verses once more imply a positive one that Yahweh has done so.

The other examples in Deutero-Isaiah[3] are of a different kind. In xlix 21 Zion's questions 'Who has borne me these?' and 'Who has brought up these?' express incredulity and hardly require an answer. In liii 1 ('Who would have believed what we have heard? and to whom has the arm of Yahweh been revealed?') the first question expresses the unbelievable character of what has been made known to the speaker: the מִי is general and impersonal. The second question has been variously interpreted; probably מִי here has the depreciatory force which it has in such phrases as 'Who am I?' and 'Who is *X*?': it expresses surprise that Yahweh's power should have been revealed to, or in connection with, such an apparently insignificant person.

---

[1] The commentators referred to in the foregoing note all agree, following Cheyne, that the text should be reconstructed in this way, with the exception of C. R. North.

[2] 40 MSS read בָּכֶם for בָּהֶם. In either case the reference is to the heathen gods.

[3] xliv 10, which is probably not the work of Deutero-Isaiah, is omitted from the discussion.

The foregoing discussion shows that the form of the questions in Isa. xl 13 f. by itself offers no solution to the problem of their intention and meaning. In addition, Deutero-Isaiah contains no precise parallels to them from which such a conclusion might be drawn. The מִי here clearly cannot refer to Yahweh, as in some of the passages which have been considered; but beyond this there is nothing to indicate which of several possible affirmations is concealed behind it.

Moreover, in view of the fact that questions of this formal type, as well as of other types, are widely scattered throughout the Old Testament and are not confined to any one literary genre, we cannot trace its literary antecedents or affinities. We can go no further than to say that in choosing this form the author was availing himself of the language of rational argument and persuasion which was common to both the daily life and the literature of Israel.[1]

B. WISDOM VOCABULARY

It has been maintained by a number of critics that verses 12–17 are deeply marked by the vocabulary and style of the wisdom tradition.[2] This argument depends to a large extent on the erroneous assumption that the use of the question form is a special characteristic of wisdom literature.[3] Apart from this,

---

[1] Westermann's distinction between *Bestreitung* and *Streitgespräch* is a technical one which does not help us here.

[2] Especially von Waldow, 'Anlaß und Hintergrund', pp. 47 ff.; 'The Message of Deutero-Isaiah', pp. 269 f.; W. McKane, *Prophets and Wise Men* (SBT **44**), London, 1965, pp. 81 f.; Fohrer and other commentaries *ad loc*. Most of these writers explain this as a simple borrowing of the style of the wise man as a technique of argument. McKane, however, regards this passage and others as examples of an anti-wisdom polemic found in the prophetical literature generally: see his section on 'The prophetic use of the vocabulary of wisdom', *op. cit.*, pp. 65–130. On the question in general, cf. J. Lindblom, 'Wisdom in the Old Testament Prophets' (*VT* Suppl. **3**, pp. 192–204).

[3] The current debate on the influence of the wisdom tradition on types of Old Testament literature not normally designated as wisdom literature, including the prophetical books, cannot be discussed here. For a list of some of the literature see J. L. Crenshaw, 'Method in Determining Wisdom Influence

the main support for this theory comes from the claim that verse 14 contains a number of specifically wisdom terms.

It is true that verse 14 contains a number of words which occur frequently, though not exclusively, in the wisdom books of the Old Testament: עֵצָה, יָעַץ, and אֹרַח and דֶּרֶךְ used in a metaphorical sense. The occurrence of three verbs meaning 'teach', even though these also are not confined to the wisdom books, might seem to confirm this view by setting the verse in the framework of the schools in which wisdom was taught.[1] But in spite of the use of these verbs, the primary reference of the verse is not to the wisdom schools, as will be demonstrated later in the discussion. In the absence of any clear agreement at present on what is meant by 'wisdom influence', it would be hazardous to assert the existence of such influence here except in a very general sense.

C. THE VOCABULARY OF POLITICS

Two phrases in particular indicate that the kind of 'wisdom' which Deutero-Isaiah has in mind here is the wisdom of the court, or more precisely the political and professional wisdom of the 'experts' who surrounded the king and whom he consulted in political affairs. These are אִישׁ עֲצָתוֹ and אֶת־מִי נוֹעָץ.

עֵצָה is, among other things, the technical term for the professional advice given to the king.[2] Preceded by אִישׁ in the construct it occurs only in two other passages: Isa. xlvi 11,

upon "Historical" Literature', *JBL* **88** (1969), pp. 129–42, esp. p. 129 n. 1). This article correctly insists that future study in this field will require a much more precise definition of wisdom than has yet been attained, and a clearer understanding of correct method in the assessment of such wisdom influences.
[1] It is frequently supposed that l 4, 'Morning by morning he wakens my ear to hear like those who are taught' (or, 'in accordance with that which is taught', according to Driver: see North, *ad loc.*) is a reference to instruction in school; but the fact that Deutero-Isaiah used this metaphor does not prove that he himself had been a pupil in a wisdom school.
[2] For a description of such a royal council meeting see especially 2 Sam. xvi 20–xvii 14. Cf. also de Boer, 'The Counsellor'; W. McKane, *Prophets and Wise Men*; R. N. Whybray, *The Succession Narrative* (SBT 2nd series **9**), London, 1968.

אִישׁ עֲצָתִי,[1] and Ps. cxix 24, אַנְשֵׁי עֲצָתִי. The example in
Isa. xlvi 11 need not detain us, since, as is almost universally
agreed, the meaning here is quite different: עֵצָה is used in the
sense not of 'counsel' but of 'purpose, plan', and the suffix
is subjective, not objective. The phrase means 'the man who
carries out my plan', and the reference is to Cyrus.[2] In
Ps. cxix 24 on the other hand the suffix is objective, and the
only possible rendering is 'thy decrees[3]... are my counsellors'.
The psalmist here refers to God's commandments by a
metaphor, as though they were God's servants assigned to
him to act as his counsellors. It is improbable that he would
have used this metaphor if he were not familiar with אִישׁ עֵצָה
as a common phrase meaning 'counsellor'. The use of the
word אִישׁ here can best be understood as having the same
force as in the phrases אִישׁ הָאֲדָמָה, a farmer, Gen. ix 20;
אִישׁ אֳנִיּוֹת, a sailor, 1 Kings ix 27; אִישׁ מִלְחָמָה, a soldier,
Joel ii 7; אִישׁ בְּשֹׂרָה, a messenger, 2 Sam. xviii 20.[4] Thus in
spite of the infrequency of the expression it is probable that
in Isa. xl 14 it denotes a professional royal counsellor, and is
similar or identical in meaning to the more frequent יוֹעֵץ.

This conclusion is supported by the phrase אֶת־מִי נוֹעָץ.
The Niphal of יָעַץ means 'hold a consultation'. But followed
by the particles אֵת, עִם or אֶל it has a more restricted sense, of
a king in consultation with his professional advisers: Reho-
boam with his 'young men' and his elders (1 Kings xii 6, 8 =
2 Chron. x 6, 8); the king of Syria and his 'servants' (2 Kings
vi 8). In Chronicles the scope of the group consulted is
sometimes widened: David consults the leaders of the nation
(1 Chron. xiii 1); Jehoshaphat 'the people' (2 Chron. xx 21);
Hezekiah his 'officers and mighty men' (2 Chron. xxxii 3).

[1] So Qere. Kethib עֲצָתוֹ.

[2] The use of the same phrase by Deutero-Isaiah in two entirely different senses
is strange. It is presumably another example of paronomasia. That the senses
are in fact different can hardly be denied.

[3] The textual problem of this verse is not relevant to the present discussion.

[4] According to *BDB* it indicates an occupation, according to Köhler (*Lexicon*)
a position or public function.

In the earlier narratives it is always the 'experts' (military or political) who are consulted; and it is important to note that the word is never used with these particles except with the king as subject. This is true even of the passages in Chronicles.[1]

D. THE VOCABULARY OF INSTRUCTION: הֵבִין, לִמַּד, הוֹדִיעַ

Everything in the previous discussion points to a picture of Yahweh as king, surrounded by a heavenly court: the question is asked whether any of its members can be said to have been needed to give him professional advice. In this context the presence of the three verbs meaning 'teach' is surprising. They hardly belong to the same sphere of ideas as the 'political' vocabulary considered above. While they can be used of the giving of authoritative *religious* instruction to kings,[2] they are never used of the advice given to a king by his counsellors, for which the regular word is the Qal of יָעַץ (e.g. 2 Sam. xvi 23).[3] It would be possible to speak of 'teaching' a young prince: King Lemuel's mother 'instructed him' (יִסְּרַתּוּ, Prov. xxxi 1), presumably when he was a child; but this is clearly not the situation envisaged here.

The three verbs overlap in meaning to some extent, although each has its own characteristics. הוֹדִיעַ is the least specialised: it is used in the sense of conveying information in general, and of instruction given by God, priests, parents and wise men.[4] לִמַּד is more specifically a word belonging to the field of education. It is often best translated 'train', and the things taught include songs, war, bad habits, foreign

---

[1] The above list of passages is exhaustive.

[2] So in 1 Sam. x 8 Samuel says that he will 'show' Saul (וְהוֹדַעְתִּי לְךָ) what to do; in 2 Chron. xxvi 5 one Zechariah instructed (מֵבִין) Uzziah in the fear of Yahweh.

[3] There are other phrases, e.g. הָבוּ לָכֶם עֵצָה, 2 Sam. xvi 20.

[4] E.g. by God, Gen. xli 39; 2 Sam. vii 21; Jer. xi 18; by Moses, Exod. xviii 16; by the priests, Ezek. xxii 26; xliv 23; by parents, Deut. iv 9; Isa. xxxviii 19; Ps. lxxviii 5; by wise men, Prov. xxii 19, 21.

languages and religious teaching.[1] הָבִין is the most specialised of the three. It is found exclusively in the later books of the Old Testament, and always denotes the giving of specifically religious teaching by God himself or by his angels, Levites, sages or other special servants.[2]

The most probable explanation of the presence of these verbs in conjunction with others which belong to a quite different sphere of ideas is that Deutero-Isaiah was here trying to create the impression of an absurd situation by a deliberate use of incongruity: not content with holding up to ridicule the idea of Yahweh as dependent on the advice of others, he uses these verbs to show how this would in fact make him inferior to his own advisers: an ignoramus, a schoolboy, one himself in need of religious instruction.[3]

It is clear from the above investigation that the scene depicted in these verses is primarily one in which Yahweh is represented as a king consulting his professional advisers before embarking upon some course of action; the similarities to the style and vocabulary of the wisdom literature are secondary to this, and do not suggest the direct influence of the wisdom schools, but rather show how far 'wisdom' and court usage coincided. It is therefore necessary for the full understanding of these verses to consider the relation of this picture of a divine court to the institution of the royal council in Israel, to other descriptions of Yahweh's court in the Old Testament, and to the concept of an assembly of the gods in the ancient Near East generally.

[1] E.g. songs, Deut. xxxi 19; Jer. ix 19; war, Judg. iii 2; 2 Sam. xxii 35; evil habits, Deut. xx 18; Jer. ix 4; a foreign language, Dan. i 4; religious teaching, Deut, iv 1; Ps. xxxiv 12; Ezra vii 10.

[2] By God, Isa. xxviii 9; Ps. cxix 27 and *passim*; Job vi 24; xxxii 8; by Gabriel, Dan. viii 16; by Levites, Neh. viii 7, 9; 2 Chron. xxxv 3; by the sons of Asaph, 1 Chron. xxv 8; by sages, Dan. xi 33; by Zechariah, Uzziah's mentor, 2 Chron. xxvi 5.

[3] For a picture of a foolish king who needs advice but will not take it, cf. Eccles. iv 13.

CHAPTER IV

ISRAELITE KINGS
AND THEIR COUNCILS

We may begin by considering what can be learned about the character and procedure of the royal council meeting as an institution of the Israelite monarchy, from which the phrase אֶת־מִי נוֹעָץ in Isa. xl 14 has been borrowed.[1] The Niphal of יָעַץ occurs 22 times in the Old Testament. Of these cases, all except 6 refer to a king's consultation with his advisers or experts. Among the non-royal cases the verb is used once absolutely and with no specific reference (Prov. xiii 10); and here it may either be reflexive (thinking a matter over) or it may refer to the taking of advice from others. In the other 4 cases (i.e. excluding Isa. xl 14) it is followed by יַחְדָּו, 'together', and means to hold a meeting to discuss problems of mutual concern or to draw up a plan of action (Isa. xlv 21; Pss. lxxi 10; lxxxiii 6; Neh. vi 7). With the king as subject it is used 3 times absolutely: in 2 cases it refers to the making of a decision (...וַיִּוָּעַץ הַמֶּלֶךְ וַיַּעַשׂ, 1 Kings xii 28; וַיִּוָּעַץ אֲמַצְיָהוּ ...וַיִּשְׁלַח..., 2 Chron. xxv 17), and as in Prov. xiii 10 may or may not imply consultation with others; in the third, in which King Hezekiah and his princes and the assembly in Jerusalem 'took counsel to keep the Passover' (2 Chron. xxx 2), the reference is to a royal council meeting, but one where the Chronicler appears to be emphasising that the decision was taken 'democratically' and not by the king alone.

In all the remaining passages[2] the king assembles his advisers or experts, and the verb נוֹעָץ is followed, as has already been noted, by one of the three particles עִם, אֶת and

[1] For a general survey of the evidence concerning the organisation of the Israelite monarchy and the king's ministers and officers see R. de Vaux, *Les Institutions de l'Ancien Testament*, vol. 1, Paris, 1958 (ET *Ancient Israel: Its Life and Institutions*, London, 1961).
[2] See the references on p. 28 above.

31

אֶל. In 2 (4) cases (1 Kings xii 6 = 2 Chron. x 6; 1 Kings xii 8 f. = 2 Chron. x 8 f.) the verb occurs a second time in the participle: the king 'takes counsel' (וַיִּוָּעֵץ) and asks them 'How/what do you advise?' (מָה/אֵיךְ אַתֶּם נוֹעָצִים), the Niphal here presumably meaning the giving of advice after mutual discussion.

These passages indicate that royal council meetings might assume a variety of forms. In the two cases where the particle אֶל is used (וַיִּוָּעֵץ אֶל־עֲבָדָיו, 2 Kings vi 8; וַיִּוָּעֵץ אֶל־הָעָם, 2 Chron. xx 21), no actual consultation is recorded. It is possible that it may have been omitted for the sake of brevity, but we are told only of the final decision, which is made by the king himself: 'He took counsel with (אֶל־) his servants, saying, "At such and such a place shall be my camp"', 2 Kings vi 8; 'And he took counsel with (אֶל־) the people and appointed...', 2 Chron. xx 21.[1] In all the other cases the particle is either עִם or אֵת, implying some measure of common deliberation, a distinction which is confirmed by the contexts. In 2 Chron. xxxii 3 Hezekiah 'consulted with (עִם) his officers and mighty men to stop the water of the springs... and they helped him'. Here we appear to have a meeting with a specific agenda in which the king and his advisers act as a committee for planning and for subsequent action. In 1 Chron. xiii 1 f. the situation is somewhat different. David proposes a plan: 'If it seems good to you, and if it is the will of Yahweh our God, let us send...' The agreement of the assembly is necessary: 'All the assembly agreed (וַיֹּאמְרוּ) to do so, for the thing was right in the eyes of all the people' (verse 4). In 1 Kings xii 6–14 and parallel the king has no proposal to make. He merely propounds the problem, first to one body of advisers (the elders) and then to another (the young men).[2] To the first he asks, 'How do you advise (me)

---

[1] Cf. the absolute use of the verb in 1 Kings xii 28: 'took counsel and made'.
[2] For the view that the 'young men' were the royal princes, and that they constituted a second regularly established body which the king was obliged to consult see A. Malamat, *Organs of Statecraft in the Israelite Monarchy*, Jerusalem, 1964.

to answer this people (לְהָשִׁיב אֶת־הָעָם־הַזֶּה דָּבָר)?' In the second case the question is more intimate: 'What do you advise that *we* (וְנָשִׁיב) should answer this people?' Then, having heard two opposite opinions, the king takes the final decision. But there has been a genuine consultation: the king allows himself to be influenced by one of the two answers, rejects the other, and gives the reply to the men of Israel in exactly the terms suggested to him by the young men.

We find a similar scene in the council meeting held by the usurper Absalom (2 Sam. xvi 20–xvii 14), a passage in which the Niphal of יָעַץ does not occur, but where יָעַץ, עֵצָה (in the Qal) and יוֹעֵץ, 'counsellor', all occur. Here again the king calls for and listens to two contrary opinions, expressed by Ahithophel and Hushai. But the procedure differs in some respects from the case considered above. The final decision is taken, not by the king alone, but by the king and the whole assembly together (xvii 14), after hearing speeches from two professional counsellors.

The above examples show that royal councils in Israel might differ considerably in character and procedure, no doubt in accordance with varying circumstances and with the character of the king concerned. These differences are to some extent indicated by differences in the use of particles: where אֶל is used, the purpose of the meeting is apparently merely to communicate a royal decision; where עִם or אֶת is used, there is always a measure of consultation. We may conclude therefore that in Isa. xl 14 Yahweh, as king, is pictured as holding a royal council; and the question asked is whether it is conceivable that he found it necessary to ask for the help and advice of one or more of its members, or of professional counsellors, before creating the world. In other words, Deutero-Isaiah is here raising the question either of the existence or of the nature of the divine council.

CHAPTER V

THE ORIGIN OF
THE DIVINE COUNCIL

This image of the divine council is not simply a poetic image
invented by Deutero-Isaiah as a means of expressing his
message more forcibly. The concept of an assembly or
council of divine beings in heaven presided over by a king or
chief god was a regular feature of the religions of the ancient
Near East from very early times. In polytheistic religions
something of the kind was almost inevitable: it was necessary
that the mutual relationships of the various gods, their
functions and their relative importance should be defined.
This could only be done on the assumption that the divine
society was organised along lines similar to the organisation
of human society.[1]

The existence of such an assembly in human society in the
ancient Near East from very early times has recently been
demonstrated.[2] The earliest type of city government in
Sumer took the form of an assembly (*unkin*) of all the free,
adult citizens, in whose hands resided ultimate sovereignty.
Rulers and magistrates were appointed by it, derived their
authority from it, and could be deposed by it. Although the
demands of efficiency and in particular the urge for foreign
conquest very quickly led to the supersession of this form
of government by the autocracy of one man who held
permanent office as king, some features of democratic government,[3] especially in judicial matters, persisted in the cities

[1] Put religiously or theologically, this would no doubt be expressed in the
opposite way: human society was modelled on divine.
[2] T. Jacobsen, 'Primitive Democracy in Ancient Mesopotamia', *JNES* **2**
(1943), pp. 159–72; 'Early Political Development in Mesopotamia', *ZA* **52**
(NF **18**) (1957), pp. 91–140; W. F. Albright, *History, Archaeology and Christian
Humanism*, London, 1965, pp. 180 ff.
[3] Albright, *op. cit.*, p. 183 n. 8, prefers the term 'gerontocracy' to Jacobsen's
'primitive democracy'.

of Mesopotamia right through the period of the great Semitic empires, and were even reinforced in the early second millennium with the arrival of new elements of Semitic population whose form of local government was of a similar character. Thus while in the period of the empires autocracy was the norm, the 'democratic' principle constantly reasserted itself to a limited extent.[1]

Concepts of divine government corresponded to the facts of human government. The Mesopotamian myths and epics mainly reflect the early period: decisions were taken by the whole assembly of the gods, and the king of the gods possessed no autocratic powers; but in *Enuma Eliš* we see a significant development: the threat of defeat by Tiamat forces the gods to confer permanent and absolute power on the strong young god Marduk in return for his protection.[2] The new situation did not, however, result in the abolition or suppression of the council of gods; rather, in a way similar to the evolution in human society, it changed its character. Not only did the other gods become subordinate to the king, charged by him with specific functions, but the council itself became a means of enhancing the magnificence of the king and praising him, and a place for giving and receiving orders, rather than one where decisions were taken jointly after debate.[3] This autocratic form of divine government did not, however, preclude the use of divine counsellors by the divine autocrat.[4]

This fluidity in the powers of the assembly or council in Mesopotamia in both the divine and the human spheres is not without relevance to the study of divine – and human – councils elsewhere in the ancient Near East. It would be rash to assume that the concept was the same in each religion, or that it remained unchanged throughout the history of any

---

[1] Albright, *op. cit.*, pp. 184 ff.
[2] *Enuma Eliš* II 127 = III 62, 120; IV 1 ff. See W. G. Lambert, 'The Reign of Nebuchadnezzar I: A Turning Point in the History of Ancient Mesopotamian Religion', *The Seed of Wisdom, Essays in Honour of T. J. Meek*, Toronto, 1964, p. 4.
[3] See *Enuma Eliš*, IV 1–15; V 77–156.
[4] See below, pp. 71–5.

35

one religion. In particular, for every area and for every period the question must be asked whether the divine council was thought of as entirely subservient to the divine king or as possessing some authority of its own. In this connection it is not without interest to observe that the fluctuation in function and authority which was observable in Mesopotamia corresponds rather closely to the variations in the function of the *royal* council in Israel which we have already discussed.

CHAPTER VI

THE ASSEMBLY OF
THE GODS IN CANAAN

Although the concept of an assembly of the gods is clearly attested in the Canaanite sources, whose relevance to the study of the background of Israelite religion is generally admitted, the nature of the evidence is unfortunately far from clear. The only detailed information comes from the Ugaritic texts, whose interpretation is seriously disputed. Consequently it is by no means certain how absolute the power of the king of the gods was held to be.

The positions of both El and Baal are ambiguous. On the one hand, El is regularly referred to as 'king'; he receives homage from the other gods, and it appears that no important step can be taken without his consent.[1] Yet he is susceptible to bullying by other gods,[2] and his authority can be flouted and his council intimidated.[3] On the other hand, Baal, who in the one passage which describes a full council meeting 'stands by El', presumably in a subordinate position,[4] yet can be hailed as king elsewhere.[5]

This dispute, or at least ambiguity, over the question of the holder of the office of king does not in any way cast doubt on the existence of the office itself, but it provides no information about the proper functions of the council in relation to

[1] E.g. Baal II iv 20 ff. (4 iv 20 ff.). References to Ugaritic texts are given as in G. R. Driver, *Canaanite Myths and Legends* (*Old Testament Studies* 3), Edinburgh, 1956. The references in brackets are to A. Herdner, *Corpus des tablettes en cunéiformes alphabétiques découvertes à Ras Shamra–Ugarit de 1929 à 1939*, Paris, 1963.
[2] Aq. III vi 7 ff. (18 i 10 ff.); Baal v v 23 ff. (3 v 3 ff.).
[3] Baal III* B 18 ff. (2 i 20 ff.).
[4] Baal III* B 19 (2 i 21).
[5] Baal II iv 43–4 (4 iv 43–4). It is denied by some writers (e.g. J. Gray, *The Legacy of Canaan*, *VT* Suppl. 5, 2nd edn, 1965, p. 155) that the application of this title to Baal is intended to imply a denial of El's permanent kingship.

those of the king. In as far as El's position is threatened, the threat comes from gods who seek to replace him. The conflicts between the gods can, therefore, not be used to interpret their normal functions as members of El's council.

In any case the pantheon reflected in the mythological texts undoubtedly differs from that which formed the object of the daily worship of the citizens of Ugarit, at any rate in historical times.[1] On the other hand the non-mythological texts which refer to the actual Ugaritic cult are too brief and too cryptic to provide clear information about the relationships between the various gods.[2] In neither group of texts is there any evidence that there was any god specifically charged with the office of counsellor, although this possibility cannot be excluded.[3]

[1] See W. F. Albright, *Yahweh and the Gods of Canaan*, London, 1968, pp. 122-6.
[2] On the whole question of the assembly of the gods at Ugarit see, *inter alia*, M. H. Pope, *El in the Ugaritic Texts* (*VT* Suppl. **2**), 1955, pp. 27-9; G. Widengren, 'Early Hebrew Myths and their Interpretation', *Myth, Ritual and Kingship*, ed. S. H. Hooke, Oxford, 1958, pp. 160-5; W. Schmidt, *Königtum Gottes in Ugarit und Israel* (B*ZAW* **80**), 1961, pp. 20 f.; Gray, *The Legacy of Canaan*, pp. 154-9; H.-J. Kraus, *Worship in Israel*, Oxford, 1966, p. 204; Albright, *Yahweh and the Gods of Canaan*, pp. 104-9. On Eissfeldt's theory (*El im ugaritischen Pantheon* (*Berichte über die Verhandlungen der sächsischen Akademie der Wissenschaften zu Leipzig*, Phil.-hist. Klasse, Band **98**, Heft 4), Berlin, 1951) that there was a tendency at Ugarit to regard El as the only god, and the other deities as merely emanations from him, see the criticisms of Pope, *op. cit.*, pp. 85–90.
[3] The god Ktr w Ḥss, although he gives advice to Baal concerning the construction of his house, hardly qualifies for such a position. He is rather a craftsman-god who makes artifacts not only for the gods (Baal's weapons and house) but also for heroes (Aqhat's bow) in the mythological texts. See Gray, *The Legacy of Canaan*, p. 189; Albright, *Yahweh and the Gods of Canaan*, pp. 118–20.

CHAPTER VII

THE COUNCIL OF YAHWEH
IN ISRAEL

The evidence so far collected[1] suggests that the nature of the divine council in Israel, to which the Old Testament contains a number of allusions, needs more study than has hitherto been devoted to it. That it was no mere poetic image, but was believed to be a reality, is now generally agreed.[2] But the status of the heavenly beings with which Yahweh was believed to be surrounded, and the degree of their power, if any, are matters which are more difficult to decide. Yet if we are to obtain a clearer idea of what the concept meant to Deutero-Isaiah and his contemporaries, the question must be investigated.

The unsolved questions here are numerous. What was the origin of the concept in Israel? Did it arise independently of foreign influence? What was its history? Was there a progressive demythologisation, with an ever-increasing movement towards a monotheistic conception?[3] How far is it necessary to take into account the possibility of a simultaneous existence of popular and more monotheistic ideas?

[1] On evidence for a 'synod of the gods' in Egypt see H. Kees, *Der Götterglaube im alten Ägypten*, Leipzig, 1941, p. 214. There seems, however, to be no evidence that this concept played an important part in Egyptian religion.

[2] H. W. Robinson, 'The Council of Yahweh', *JTS* 45 (1944), pp. 151–7; *Inspiration and Revelation in the Old Testament*, Oxford, 1946, pp. 167–70. His thesis has been accepted by F. M. Cross, 'The Council of Yahweh in Second Isaiah', *JNES* 12 (1953), pp. 274–8; A. R. Johnson, *Sacral Kingship in Ancient Israel*, Cardiff, 1955, *passim*; R. E. Brown, 'The Pre-Christian Semitic Concept of "Mystery"', *CBQ* 20 (1958), pp. 417–20; H.-J. Kraus, 'Die Kulttraditionen Jerusalems', *Psalmen*, vol. 1 (Biblische Kommentar), 1961, pp. 197–205; G. Cooke, 'The Sons of (the) God(s)', *ZAW* 76 (1964), pp. 22–47; Albright, *Yahweh and the Gods of Canaan*, pp. 166 f., and other writers.

[3] So e.g. H. Ringgren, *Israelitische Religion*, Stuttgart, 1963, pp. 84 f. (ET *Israelite Religion*, Philadelphia, 1966, pp. 95 f.); Cooke, *art. cit.*; Albright, *Yahweh and the Gods of Canaan*, pp. 159 f.

The similarity of the Old Testament terminology to that of both Mesopotamia and Canaan has frequently been pointed out.[1] The expressions בְּנֵי (הָ)אֱלֹהִים (Gen. vi 2; Job i 6; ii 1; xxxviii 7); בְּנֵי אֵלִים (Ps. xxix 1; lxxxix 7); בְּנֵי עֶלְיוֹן (Ps. lxxxii 6); קְדֹשִׁים (Deut. xxxiii 3); סוֹד־קְדֹשִׁים (Ps. lxxxix 8); סוֹד אֱלוֹהַ (Job xv 8); סוֹד יהוה (Jer. xxiii 18, 22); עֲדַת־אֵל (Ps. lxxxii 1); קְהַל קְדֹשִׁים (Ps. lxxxix 6) clearly have their counterparts in Accadian *puḫur ilāni* and Ugaritic *qdšm, bn qdš, dr il, dr bn il, pḫr ilm, pḫr bn ilm, mpḫrt bn il*.[2] The fact that many other similarities exist between Ugaritic and Old Testament mythological and religious terminology confirms this.[3] Moreover in Ps. xcv 3 it is expressly stated that Yahweh is 'the great king over all the gods'.

These similarities of terminology, which are especially close in the case of Canaan and Israel, do not necessarily imply that the concept of the divine assembly itself arose in Israel in direct imitation of Canaanite models. W. F. Albright has recently argued[4] that in view of the antiquity of the concept in the ancient Near East there is no reason to suppose this. Other writers[5] have suggested that some such

[1] See, *inter alia*, the works listed on p. 38 n. 2 and p. 39 n. 2 above, and also J. H. Patton, *Canaanite Parallels in the Book of Psalms*, Baltimore, 1944, p. 24.

[2] Cf. also *kl dr bn 'lm* in the Phoenician (Karatepe) Inscription of Azitawadda (H. Donner and W. Röllig, *Kanaanäische und Aramäische Inschriften*, Wiesbaden, 1964, vol. I, nr. **26**, A III 19; translation in *ANET*, p. 500). For the suggestion that דּוֹר in Hebrew may in some cases have the meaning of 'assembly', and that in particular דָּרֶךְ in Amos viii 14 should be pointed דֹּרְךָ and translated 'thy pantheon', referring to a group of deities worshipped at Beersheba, see F. J. Neuberg, 'An Unrecognized Meaning of Hebrew *DÔR*', *JNES* **9** (1950), pp. 215–17; P. R. Ackroyd, 'The Meaning of Hebrew דּוֹר Considered', *JSS* **13** (1968), pp. 3–10.

It should be noted that R. Rendtorff ('El, Ba'al und Jahwe', *ZAW* **78** (1966), pp. 277–92), following W. Herrmann, denies that the Ugaritic expressions *dr bn il, pḫr bn ilm* and the like (or their Canaanite and Phoenician equivalents) refer to the whole pantheon. He points out that in the Ugaritic texts Baal has his own *pḫr b'l*, and argues that the other expressions similarly refer simply to a particular group of deities dependent on one or another god. See especially Patton, *Canaanite Parallels*.

[4] *Yahweh and the Gods of Canaan*, p. 167.

[5] A. R. Johnson, *The One and the Many in the Israelite Conception of God*, Cardiff, 1942, ²1961, p. 16; Robinson, *Inspiration and Revelation*, p. 170; G. E. Wright, *The Old Testament Against Its Environment* (SBT **2**), London, 1950, pp. 30 ff.

concept was almost inevitable: in the ancient Near East the idea of any person, whether human or divine, existing in loneliness and isolation was inconceivable: like anyone else, a god of Yahweh's status would quite naturally be thought to have his 'household'.

Nevertheless the terminology makes it probable that Israel was at least influenced by its Canaanite neighbours in the way in which it expressed the concept;[1] and the use of such expressions as בְּנֵי אֵלִים, whatever new meaning may have been attached to them, obviously created the danger of a frankly polytheistic interpretation.

That polytheism was practised in Israel at various times cannot be doubted. The worship of the Canaanite gods Baal and Asherah was introduced at an early stage (Judges vi), and that of Phoenician deities in the northern kingdom during the reign of Ahab; and in Judah from the time of Ahaz onwards those kings who acknowledged the suzerainty of Assyria or Babylonia especially encouraged polytheism (2 Kings xxi 3 ff.; Jer. vii 18; xliv 17-19, 25; Zeph. i 4-9). Such worship was practised during the reign of Manasseh and during the last years of the monarchy even in the Temple of Jerusalem itself (2 Kings xxiii; Ezek. viii). Since the years which preceded the exile were among those when these practices were at their height, it might be supposed that the Babylonian exiles took with them into exile a concept of Yahweh among the gods very different from the concept of God for which the prophets had stood.

Yet there is little, if any, evidence in the Old Testament that this worship of other gods than Yahweh took the form of an organised polytheistic system in which Yahweh, like El at

---

[1] For various theories on this subject, including the possibility of Canaanite influence on the Israelite cult at Jerusalem see the works mentioned above and also, *inter alia*, H. H. Rowley, 'Melchizedek and Zadok', *Festschrift Alfred Bertholet*, Tübingen, 1950, pp. 461-72; *Worship in Ancient Israel*, London, 1967, pp. 71 ff.; H. Schmid, 'Jahwe und die Kulttraditionen von Jerusalem', *ZAW* **67** (1955), pp. 168-97; G. W. Ahlström, *Aspects of Syncretism in Israelite Religion*, Lund, 1963; R. E. Clements, *God and Temple*, Oxford, 1965, pp. 40 ff.

Ugarit or Marduk at Babylon, was regarded as presiding over a society of gods each with his own name, characteristics and clearly defined powers and functions, to whom worship might be offered. Evidently some Israelites worshipped other gods as well as Yahweh, while others may have abandoned the worship of Yahweh in favour of other cults. But all the texts which speak specifically of the divine council clearly regard Yahweh as alone possessing absolute power, and in no case is any member of the council given a name or a distinct personality. There is no direct evidence in the Old Testament of a pantheon in the sense in which the concept was first understood outside Israel.[1]

The worship of the 'host of heaven' (צבא השמים) sometimes mentioned together with that of the sun and moon, which was practised in the latter days of the monarchy[2] was an astral cult which, in spite of its identity with one of the terms used in the ninth century for the council of Yahweh (1 Kings xxii 19), was an innovation introduced probably under Assyrian and Babylonian influence, and was practised in clear distinction from the worship of Yahweh, either side by side with it or as an alternative to it. It is true that Deut. iv 19 (cf. xxix 25) seems to imply that in some circles it was believed that it was permissible for the foreign nations to worship the host of heaven, or even that such worship was ordained by Yahweh for them; but the idea is not fully developed, and occurs only here. Elsewhere in Deuteronomy (xvii 2–7) such worship is described as an 'abomination' (תועבה) when practised by Israelites. This is a very strong word to use of a practice which in other circumstances had divine approval. The thought expressed in these verses is

---

[1] The occurrence of the names Herembethel, Eshembethel, Anathbethel and Anathyahu side by side with Yahu (= Yahweh) as divine names in the Elephantine Papyri has often been taken as evidence that a pantheon with Yahweh at its head must have existed in Palestine at the time when the ancestors of the Jewish community there emigrated from their homeland. But this is not the only possible explanation of the evidence. See E. G. Kraeling, *The Brooklyn Museum Aramaic Papyri*, Yale, 1953, pp. 83–91.

[2] Deut. iv 19; xvii 3; 2 Kings xxi 2–5; xxiii 4 f.; Jer. viii 2; Zeph. i 5.

probably an incidental speculation rather than the considered statement of a clearly defined belief. In any case the cult of the host of heaven is never spoken of in association with that of Yahweh; on the other hand, it is frequently mentioned together with the worship of 'other gods' who have nothing in common with him.[1] In 2 Kings xxiii 4 f. it is expressly associated with Baal and Asherah.

The phrase itself refers to the stars,[2] probably including the sun and moon when these are not specifically mentioned. The stars are in the Old Testament always regarded as created and controlled by Yahweh,[3] and, like all other creatures, are capable of giving praise to him (Ps. cxlviii 2–4). Since their place was in heaven it was natural that they should sometimes be identified with Yahweh's heavenly council.[4]

The statement in Isa. xxiv 21 that 'on that day Yahweh will punish the host of heaven, in heaven'[5] appears to be a late poetical reference to a myth concerning a struggle between heavenly powers. This myth, or a related one, may also be that referred to in Isa. xiv 12 ff., where fallen Babylon is represented as the Morning Star, Son of Dawn (Shachar) who tried to gain supremacy over the 'sons of El' but was cast down from heaven, a story which in turn appears to have affinities with some themes in the Ugaritic mythology.[6]

[1] Deut. xvii 3; 2 Kings xxi 3; xxiii 4 f. The meaning of Zeph. i 4 f., where the worship of Yahweh is mentioned together with that of the host of heaven and of Milcom (following a probable emendation), is not clear, but it does not suggest that the host of heaven was regarded as a pantheon headed by Yahweh.

[2] In Jer. xxxiii 22 it is used of them with no specifically religious implications; cf. Gen. xv 5; xxii 17; xxvi 4; Exod. xxxii 13; Deut. i 10; xxviii 62; 1 Chron. xxvii 23; Neh. ix 23.

[3] Gen. i 14–18; ii 1; Neh. ix 6; Job xxv 5; Ps. xxxiii 6; Isa. xl 26; xlv 12; Dan. iv 32.

[4] 1 Kings xxii 19; also Job xxxviii 7, where they are linked with the בני אלהים as shouting for joy at the creation. See J. Gray, *I and II Kings* (OTL), London, 1964 on 1 Kings xxii 19 and his article 'Host of Heaven' in Hastings' *Dictionary of the Bible* (2nd edn), Edinburgh, 1963.

[5] Here the word is מרום, not שמים.

[6] See Gray, *The Legacy of Canaan*, pp. 169–71; Albright, *Yahweh and the Gods of Canaan*, pp. 198 f., 201 f.

Dan. viii 10 may be a further reference to this myth. But these allusions to myths which may never have been regarded in Israel as more than poetic tales provide no grounds for belief in an Israelite pantheon.

Two other texts have, however, been thought to refer to the existence of a pantheon in Israel at some stage in its religious development.

In Ps. lxxxii it is stated that Elohim, who in the 'Elohistic Psalter' is to be identified with Yahweh, stands up in the עדת־אל, among the 'gods' (אלהים) (verse 1), also referred to as the בני עליון (verse 6), and judges them, pronouncing sentence and taking away their immortal status. This psalm has been interpreted in many different ways. The great majority of interpreters[1] hold that Yahweh in this psalm is identical with El and Elyon, and that he acts as judge by virtue of his headship of the council. Eissfeldt, however,[2] has argued that the עדת־אל is the divine council not of Yahweh but of the god El (also called Elyon), and that Yahweh is a subordinate member of the council who has been entrusted with the task of pronouncing judgement on the others.

A similar problem exists with regard to Deut. xxxii 8 f. In this text, where a Qumran fragment has now yielded the reading בני אלהים, confirming a long standing conjecture based on LXX's 'angels of God' that the traditional Hebrew text's 'sons of Israel' is a corruption of an original 'sons of god',[3] Eissfeldt argued[4] that Elyon, who 'fixed the bounds of

[1] E.g. J. Morgenstern, 'The Mythological Background of Psalm 82', *HUCA* **14** (1939), pp. 29–126; Robinson, 'The Council of Yahweh', p. 155; Wright, *The Old Testament against its Environment*, pp. 35 f.; R. T. O'Callaghan, 'A Note on the Canaanite Background of Psalm 82', *CBQ* **15** (1953), pp. 311–14; Johnson, *Sacral Kingship*, pp. 89 f.; Brown, *CBQ* **20** (1958), p. 420; Kraus, *Psalmen*, vol. II *ad loc.*; Ringgren, *Israelitische Religion*, pp. 39 f. (ET, p. 44); Cooke, 'The Sons of (the) God(s)', pp. 29–34.

[2] 'El and Yahweh', *JSS* **I** (1956), pp. 25–37 (= 'El und Jahwe', *Kleine Schriften*, vol. III, Tübingen, 1966, pp. 386–97); followed by Schmidt, *Königtum Gottes in Ugarit und Israel*, p. 70 n. 32.

[3] P. W. Skehan, 'Qumran and the Present State of Old Testament Text Studies: The Masoretic Text', *JBL* **78** (1959), p. 21; W. F. Albright, 'Some Remarks on the Song of Moses', *VT* **9** (1959), p. 343.

[4] 'El and Yahweh', p. 29; also Schmidt, *Königtum Gottes in Ugarit und Israel*.

the peoples according to the number of the sons of God' is distinct from and superior to Yahweh, who, as a member of his entourage, received Jacob (Israel) from him as his portion (verse 9). Here again the majority of interpreters hold that Elyon in verse 8 is to be identified with Yahweh in verse 9: it was Yahweh who assigned each nation to one of the 'sons of God', retaining Israel for his own particular care.[1]

Eissfeldt qualifies his opinion that the idea of an El pantheon lies behind these two passages by an admission that the concept was a more or less meaningless survival. The idea of El as superior to Yahweh had already ceased to have any real importance for Israelites: 'at least for Israel, Yahweh was the only real God'.

Even if we can accept the view that in the course of the early development of Yahwism Yahweh succeeded to El as the head of a pantheon, this does not necessarily mean that the concept continued to have reality for the Israelites. If the transfer of the qualities and functions of El took place, as Eissfeldt holds, precisely because for Israel Yahweh was the only true God, his supersession of El as supreme divine being ought necessarily to have involved the degradation of the other 'gods', even if the traditional language continued to be used, to the status of completely subordinate beings.[2]

In fact, however, it is improbable that Eissfeldt's interpretation is correct. Both passages render a satisfactory sense on the assumption that, as elsewhere in the Old Testament, the divine names El and Elyon have already become appellations of Yahweh. The retention of references, however weakened

---

[1] See, *inter alia*, Albright, 'Some Remarks', p. 343, for a defence of this identification on stylistic grounds; Ahlström, *Aspects of Syncretism in Israelite Religion*, pp. 73 f.; and R. Meyer, 'Die Bedeutung von Deuteronomium xxxii 8 f., 43 (4Q) für die Auslegung des Mosesliedes', *Verbannung und Heimkehr, Festschrift für Wilhelm Rudolph*, Tübingen, 1961, pp. 197–209, for a fuller criticism of Eissfeldt's position.

[2] If such a process did in fact take place, Ps. lxxxii might be interpreted as a dramatic representation of Yahweh's rejection of their claim to divine status. But see below.

their sense might have become, to an older belief that Yahweh was a subordinate of El and a member of his pantheon, is extremely improbable in texts which are clearly intended to lay emphasis on the greatness of Yahweh. Both passages are more naturally seen as reflecting a stage in Israel's religious development when Yahweh, previously understood primarily as the God of Israel and of Israel's land, was coming to be recognised as supreme over the gods of the other nations. This is expressed in Deut. xxxii 8 f. by a claim that these 'gods' are merely his servants: it was he who had allotted the territories of the nations to them in the first place, and set his servants over them. It is expressed in Ps. lxxxii by a dramatic scene in which he accuses these beings of misuse of their powers, and removes them altogether from their functions.

These two texts go further than any others[1] in assigning distinct functions to these subordinate beings; but they must be understood in the light of their purpose, which was to dissuade the Israelites from believing that the 'gods' of the heathen nations were genuine deities worthy of worship. This no doubt implies that there was at some time a *tendency* to see Yahweh as the head of a pantheon; but there is no evidence that such a concept ever took concrete form.

In all the texts which we have considered there is a deliberate minimising and generalising of these subordinate beings. Indeed, one of the most striking features of the references to the divine council in comparison with the mythological texts of Canaan and Mesopotamia is the vagueness of the terms in which it is described, and the variety of the terminology employed to designate its members. This may well indicate the absence of a fixed tradition, which in turn may suggest that the concept, though a persistent one, did not occupy a central position in Israel's religious beliefs. The members of the council never come to life as real personalities. They have no names, no individual characteristics, no history and no permanent and distinctive

---

[1] On Deut. iv 19; xxix 25 see pp. 42 f., above.

functions.[1] There are no mythological details such as are found in the Mesopotamian and Ugaritic texts: no heavenly banquets, no loves, hates or other social relationships between the individual members. On occasion, members may be despatched, as in the non-Israelite myths, as messengers or agents to perform specific tasks (1 Kings xxii; Isa. vi), but fundamentally the concept is simply one of an assembly, not of a fully developed divine society. The only relationships described are between it as a body and its head, Yahweh: the members have no relationships with one another. The council exists to praise Yahweh, to fear him and to submit to his rule and judgement and to do his will.

The function of praise is referred to in a variety of texts: Deut. xxxiii 2; Job xxxviii 7; Ps. xxix 1; ciii 20–2; Isa. vi. Ps. xcv 3 simply states Yahweh's supremacy: he is 'a great God above all gods'. Deut. xxxii 8 f. refers to the heavenly beings as appointed by Yahweh to assist him in his rule over the world. In Ps. lxxxix 6–8 their fear of him is stressed, and in Ps. lxxxii his power to punish and depose them. They are in fact to all intents and purposes no more than angels.

Unfortunately the texts offer little evidence concerning the history of the concept, its progress, decline or transformation. Many of the relevant passages occur in compositions concerning whose dates there is wide disagreement,[2] and any reconstruction of the course of development is therefore bound to be speculative. Zech. iii 1 ff., concerning whose date there is no dispute, does show, however, that the concept persisted into the early post-exilic period, and its reappearance in Daniel[3] and later Jewish literature as a company of angels surrounding God's throne and acting as

---

[1] The Satan in Job i; ii has a distinctive function, but this rather marks the beginning of a later doctrine of angels, clearly seen in Daniel, according to which their functions were differentiated. Such differentiation does not appear in the earlier texts.

[2] E.g. Deut. xxxii; xxxiii and the passages from Psalms and Job. For example, opinions on the date of Ps. lxxxii range from the tenth century (Eissfeldt) to the fifth (Morgenstern).

[3] Dan. vii 9 ff.; cf. x 13, 20, 21.

his agents makes it probable that it persisted without a break in one form or another throughout the period of the Old Testament.

It is against this background of the consistent emphasis of the Old Testament texts on Yahweh's entire supremacy over his council that we may now study more closely some texts of particular relevance to Isa. xl 13 f. In these passages, although the verb יעץ and its cognates do not occur, the council of Yahweh is portrayed as a deliberative assembly in which Yahweh asks for or receives advice from the members.

CHAPTER VIII

YAHWEH AND HIS ADVISERS

In Micaiah's vision in 1 Kings xxii 19–22 (= 2 Chron. xviii 18–21) Yahweh is seated on his throne surrounded by the 'heavenly host' (כָּל־צְבָא הַשָּׁמַיִם). He introduces the subject for discussion, which concerns the history of Israel at a particular moment.

The question מִי יְפַתֶּה אֶת־אַחְאָב is usually translated 'Who will entice Ahab...?'; but in view of the statement in the next verse that there followed a discussion on the subject, it is more probable that this is one of those passages where מִי should be translated, 'How, what?',[1] and the whole phrase 'How shall one entice?', or possibly 'Who knows how to entice?'. Yahweh is thus seeking advice on a particular question, and the members of the assembly make various suggestions: 'one said one thing, and another said another'.[2] Finally 'a spirit' (הָרוּחַ) offers a suitable plan: he will go himself and entice Ahab. Yahweh puts a further question: 'By what means?' (בַּמָּה). The volunteer explains his plan,

---

[1] In Amos vii 2, מִי יָקוּם יַעֲקֹב can hardly mean anything other than 'How can Jacob stand?'. In Judg. xiii 17 מִי שְׁמֶךָ is the equivalent of the more usual מַה־שְּׁמֶךָ (e.g. Gen. xxxii 28). In Ruth iii 16 Naomi's question to her daughter מִי־אַתְּ cannot mean 'Who are you?', but is evidently an enquiry how she fared. (Cf. also Gen. xxxiii 8 and possibly Song of Sol. iii 6.) In Isa. li 19 the text is uncertain. The Massoretic reading מִי אֲנַחֲמֵךְ can hardly mean anything other than 'How shall I comfort thee?', but DSS Isa.ᴬ has the verb in the 3rd person: מִי ינחמך, 'Who shall comfort thee?'. This makes better sense in the context. That מִי in Hebrew sometimes has the same meaning as מַה is recognised by Bauer–Leander 33 a (less clearly in G.-K. 37 a) and by G. R. Driver, *Canaanite Myths and Legends*, p. 162 n. 12, and is attested in Ugaritic (Driver, *ibid.*). In Ethiopic, *mī* always means 'what?', never 'who?'.

[2] There are corruptions in both Kings and Chronicles, but the meaning is quite clear. It is probably best to follow the text preserved in Kings, but reading כָּכָה (following Chronicles here) in place of בְּכֹה, and אָמַר instead of אֹמֵר.

Yahweh makes the decision approving it, and the volunteer is sent off armed with the executive power to carry it out.

In Job i 6–12; ii 1–7 the question is one concerning the moral government of the world. The council meeting is apparently a regular one, and the assembly consists of the בְּנֵי הָאֱלֹהִים. Here Yahweh is dependent both for information and advice on the Satan, who is presumably a member of the assembly. In i 6–12 the Satan, like the four horsemen in Zech. i 8 ff.,[1] has patrolled the earth and now makes his report. Yahweh then proposes a particular subject for discussion: the case of the man Job. He gives his estimate of Job's character, but the Satan contradicts this view, and even appears to criticise Yahweh's methods. He then makes a practical suggestion. The scene ends with Yahweh's accepting the Satan's proposal. It is, however, he who makes the final decision: the Satan is sent off to carry out his proposal, but only within certain limits set by Yahweh. The second scene (ii 1–7) is similar to the first: the report, the raising of the problem, the criticism and practical suggestion, finally the commission accompanied by restrictions.

The scene in Isa. vi is somewhat different. Isaiah, like Micaiah, is allowed to observe the heavenly council meeting. Only the seraphim are mentioned as present. The scene is this time mainly concerned with the situation and mission of the prophet, who actually participates in the meeting. It is not clear whether some discussion has taken place before his arrival, which has led to a decision that someone must be sent. The first words which the prophet hears are Yahweh's question, 'Whom shall I send, and who will go for us?'. The 'for us' (לָנוּ) may or may not imply that the decision is a joint one; this point does not appear to have interested the prophet. The 'I' of Yahweh certainly implies, as in the other scenes, that the final decision is that of Yahweh alone. The prophet himself, apart from his offer to be Yahweh's messenger, offers him no advice: his question in verse 11 is

----

[1] Cf. also the seven eyes of Yahweh in Zech. iv 10.

merely for further information. He is sent off on his mission in much the same way as the messengers in the other scenes.

The scene in Zech. iii 1 ff. is a heavenly judgement scene, with Yahweh as judge, the High Priest Joshua as the accused, the Satan as prosecuting counsel, and the angel of Yahweh and others (undefined, verses 4 f.) also present. Here again the prophet is only allowed to witness the final moments of the trial. Yahweh has already taken the decision to acquit Joshua, and is engaged in rebuking the Satan. Nevertheless it is clear that as in the scene in Job, Yahweh has listened to the advice of the Satan before making his decision, even though he has rejected it.

Finally we must examine the meaning of the word סוֹד as used in connection with Yahweh.

The word סוֹד occurs 21 times in the Old Testament: it is used 13 times of human activity, 7 in connection with God, and once in connection with the 'holy ones' (קְדשִׁים). In human relations it may mean a casual or social friendly gathering (Jer. vi 11; xv 17), or 'friendship, intimacy, company' (Ps. lv 15; Job xix 19); but it also signifies a more formal meeting (Gen. xlix 6, parallel with קָהָל; Ezek. xiii 9, referring to the total number of the chosen people; Ps. cxi 1, parallel with עֵדָה). It is also used of the discussions which take place and the decisions made at meetings held for the transaction of specific business: the plots of evil-doers (Ps. lxiv 3;[1] lxxxiii 4, where הֶעֱרִים סוֹד is parallel with הִתְיָעֵץ, 'consult together'); consultation in general (Prov. xv 22, where lack of consultation, אֵין סוֹד, is contrasted with 'many counsellors', רֹב יוֹעֲצִים). In Prov. xi 13; xx 19; xxv 9, where warnings are given about the folly of 'revealing' סוֹד, it refers either to conversations or decisions made in private meetings, or to secrets confided by one person to another.

The fact that סוֹד, when used of human affairs, is some-

---

[1] In this passage it is not specifically stated that more than one person is involved in any one plot; but the similarity to Ps. lxxxiii 4, where the parallelism makes this certain, makes it unlikely that the word can mean simply 'plan'.

thing which always involves more than one person, and often refers to assemblies and meetings, must be taken into account when we consider the meaning of the סוֹד of Yahweh or of God. In this connection, most of the meanings noted above reappear: the word is used of God's intimacy or friendship with men (Ps. xxv 14, parallel with בְּרִית; Job xxix 4, parallel with 'when Shaddai was still with me'; Prov. iii 32, contrasted with 'abomination to Yahweh'). In Amos iii 7 ('Surely the Lord God does nothing without revealing (כִּי אִם־גָּלָה) his סוֹד to his servants the prophets') we have the same expression as in Prov. xi 13; xx 19; xxv 9. Here the expression might be interpreted as referring to decisions made by Yahweh alone and then revealed in private to the prophets, were it not for passages like Jer. xxiii 18, 22, where the expression עָמַד בְּסוֹד יהוה, referring to an experience apparently regarded by Jeremiah as an essential qualification of a true prophet, leaves no doubt that what is referred to is a heavenly council meeting to which prophets are admitted to stand around the divine throne with the other courtiers and hear Yahweh's words. The same concept is probably referred to in Job xv 8: 'Have you listened in the סוֹד of God?'

Such an assembly is also clearly referred to in Ps. lxxxix 8. Here, after asking who among the heavenly beings (בְּנֵי אֵלִים) can be compared to Yahweh, the Psalmist continues, 'God (אֵל) is feared in the council of the holy ones (בְּסוֹד־קְדֹשִׁים), great and terrible above all who surround him'.

A number of conclusions may be drawn from the above discussion.

(1) There existed in Israel both before and after the time of Deutero-Isaiah a concept of an assembly or council of heavenly beings who surrounded Yahweh and formed his court. He did not reign in 'splendid isolation', but had his 'household' in heaven.

(2) Whether this concept was native to Israel or not, it was sometimes expressed in terminology borrowed or adapted

from Canaan and possibly also from other foreign mythologies. The use of this terminology did not, however, necessarily imply that the meaning attached to it was the same.

(3) In Israel these heavenly beings did not constitute a pantheon. The relevant texts unanimously assert that Yahweh's supremacy is not in any way challenged by them. Their function is to praise him and do his bidding, and they may be deposed by him from their immortal status.

(4) The belief in Yahweh's absolute supremacy did not prevent the Israelites from conceiving Yahweh's council on the analogy of the councils of human kings, in which the ruler, without sacrificing any of his prerogative, might when he wished deliberate with the members before taking action.

CHAPTER IX

THE OFFICE OF COUNSELLOR

It must now be asked whether there is not some more specific
idea in the mind of Deutero-Isaiah in these verses. He refers
to an אִישׁ עֵצָה, a 'counsellor'. This might suggest that he is
referring to some belief in the existence of a specific office of
counsellor, held by an individual member of the court.[1]

We have seen that no such office is referred to in the texts
which we have considered. But some interpreters have maintained that there are texts in the Old Testament which refer
to it. Most of these passages occur in the poem of Job, whose
author, like Deutero-Isaiah, is concerned to affirm with the
greatest possible emphasis that there is no limit to the knowledge and power of God, and who refers to the idea of limitation only to refute it.

> Job xv 7 Were you the first man to be born?
>   Or were you brought forth before the hills?
>   8 Have you listened in the סוֹד of God?
>   Or do you lay exclusive claim[2] to wisdom?

There are here four questions; and it is not possible *a priori* to
decide whether they express four distinct but similar ideas, or
two pairs of identical ideas, or whether there is a progression
from one thought to the next. Verse 7*b* taken by itself
appears to be a reference to wisdom, since the words לִפְנֵי
גְבָעוֹת חוֹלָלְתָּ are identical, apart from the change from first to
second person, with the words in which personified wisdom
refers to her origins in Prov. viii 25*b*. Verse 8*a* taken by itself
might simply be a mocking suggestion by the speaker,
Eliphaz, that Job is exceptionally wise because he has been

---

[1] As was, for example, Ahithophel, although he is referred to as יוֹעֵץ, not
אִישׁ עֵצָה.

[2] On this translation see p. 55 n. 2 below.

privileged, like the prophets and certain other exceptional persons of the past, to be present at God's council.

Verse 7a, however, refers to the 'first man' (רִאישׁוֹן אָדָם (Qere)); and since the context appears to imply a belief that the first man was exceptionally wise, it has been maintained by a number of scholars that all four lines refer to a myth concerning a 'primordial man' (Urmensch)[1] who was created before the world, and who 'stole'[2] wisdom from the gods.

Some other passages in Job have been thought to refer to the same myth. In Job xxxviii 21 God mocks Job's pretensions, saying to him:

> You know, for you were born then,
> and the number of your days is great!

This verse, together with other phrases like 'for (surely) you know!' (xxxviii 5), suggests the possibility that the whole list of questions in chapters xxxviii–xxxix in which God demands whether Job has the knowledge and power to have created and sustained the world is not simply rhetoric unrelated to antecedent traditions, but a further reference to the same primordial man. The question is a complex one. It seems that there is insufficient evidence to prove direct dependence on any extant myth, though the apparent stress on the wisdom of the first man suggests a version of the paradise myth which is different from Gen. ii and close to Ezek. xxviii 11 ff. But even though this primordial man may have been believed to have acquired superhuman wisdom, and so to have become superior to ordinary mortals, there is nothing to connect him directly with the act of the creation of the world or to suggest that it was he who was believed to have been God's adviser.

[1] E.g. W. Schencke, *Die Chokma (Sophia) in der jüdischen Hypostasenspekulation*, Kristiana, 1913, pp. 7–15, 73–7; Fohrer, *Das Buch Hiob*, *ad loc*. For other literature on this subject see Fohrer, p. 268 n. 4.

[2] גָּרַע is used of cutting off or snipping off the beard in Isa. xv 2; Jer. xlviii 37. Dhorme (*Le livre de Job*, *ad loc*.) suggests that with the complement אֵלֶיךָ it means 'have you arrogated to yourself?' and so 'do you have a monopoly of?'; but a reference to a mythical event is compatible with the Hebrew.

But there are other passages in Job which might be interpreted as referring to the counsellor, and even to a person supposedly superior to the creator god.

xxxiv 13 Who charged him with (פָּקַד עָלָיו) the earth,
and who laid (שָׂם) [upon him] the whole world?
xxxvi 23 Who charged him with (פָּקַד עָלָיו) his way,
or who said to him, 'you have done wrong'?

In these verses, whether פָּקַד עַל־ means 'to assign a task' to someone, or 'to hold responsible' for something, there may be here a reference – introduced, as in the other passages, only to deny its truth – to a belief in a being superior to God, although there is no reason to identify this being with the *Urmensch*. Another such passage is Job xxi 22:

$$\text{הַלְאֵל יְלַמֶּד־דָּעַת}$$
$$\text{וְהוּא רָמִים יִשְׁפּוֹט}$$

This is translated by RSV as follows:

Will any teach God knowledge,
seeing that he judges those that are on high?

The relationship between the two lines is quite clear: the first line raises the question whether there is anyone so superior to God that he could be his teacher, only to exclude the possibility of such a thing in the second line by an *a fortiori* argument expressed in the form of a circumstantial clause:[1] he who רָמִים יִשְׁפּוֹט cannot possibly be in need of instruction.

There is, however, a divergence of opinion concerning the identity of the supposed teacher (an impersonal 3rd person in the Hebrew): it may refer to men or to divine beings. The question turns on the meaning of רָמִים, and to a lesser extent on that of יִשְׁפּוֹט. Some commentators hold that רָמִים refers to powerful or arrogant men. This is a possible meaning of

---

[1] See G.-K. 142 d for this use of וְהוּא.

רָם, and on this interpretation the question in the first line refers to the absurdity of human beings thinking themselves to be wiser than God. But 'judging the arrogant' does not constitute a very convincing proof of superior knowledge in the judge; and for this reason some commentators[1] consider that רָמִים here means 'the heavenly beings'. The word is used of the divine nature absolutely in Ps. cxxxviii 6; in the phrase רָם וְנִשָּׂא in Isa. vi 1 and also in Isa. lvii 15, where it probably refers to God's dwelling in heaven (the next line has מָרוֹם וְקָדוֹשׁ אֶשְׁכּוֹן); and in the phrase 'high above the nations' in Ps. xcix 2; cxiii 4, where the ideas of dwelling in heaven and of divine power may be combined. It is therefore entirely appropriate as an epithet of divinity.

The possibility that Job xxi 22 refers to God's superiority over other divine beings is, perhaps, somewhat strengthened by the possibility that יִשְׁפּוֹט means not 'judges' but 'rules'.[2] If, then, the whole line may be translated 'even though it is he who rules over the heavenly beings', it constitutes a logical argument that he whose power is supreme in the universe can hardly be less supreme when it comes to knowledge. This then means that the first line refers to the possibility – dismissed as an absurdity – that there should be divine beings capable of teaching knowledge to God; and the line can then be seen to be extremely close in meaning to Isa. xl 13 f., and close also in vocabulary: in both passages the verb לִמַּד is used.

References to other heavenly beings forming God's court are found elsewhere in the poem of Job, though here also the author's purpose is to assert God's complete superiority over them: according to xv 15 he 'does not trust' (לֹא יַאֲמִין) his holy ones, and 'the heavens are not pure in his sight'. According to xxv 2 f. he is represented as a conqueror

---

[1] E.g. Fohrer.
[2] It is so translated by G. Hölscher, *Das Buch Hiob* (HAT), 2nd edn, 1952, *ad loc*. That the verb may be capable of this meaning is suggested by the use of the participle in the sense of 'ruler' in Ugaritic and Punic, and perhaps also in Hebrew, e.g. Mic. iv 14.

possessing 'dominion and fear' in heaven and 'making peace' by means of his innumerable 'troops' (גְּדוּדָיו).

References to a being superior to God have also been found in Job xxviii, a poem of different authorship from that of the poem of Job, as may be clearly seen from the fact that here the concept of a divine or semi-divine being other than God is introduced not in order to be refuted or by way of allusion, but positively and of serious purpose. The reference here is not to the *Urmensch* but to wisdom.[1] There has been much discussion of verse 27, which states that God – who alone knows the way to wisdom – רָאָה וַיְסַפְּרָהּ הֱכִינָהּ וְגַם־חֲקָרָהּ. No satisfactory solution has yet been found which makes good sense of all four verbs.

רָאָה, 'see', normally implies that the thing seen existed before the act of seeing. On the other hand, followed by the particle בְּ it frequently means to look upon with especial favour or disfavour; in Gen. xxii 8 (אֱלֹהִים יִרְאֶה־לֹּו הַשֶּׂה), with the direct object, the meaning comes close to 'choose'.[2]

סְפֵּר in the Old Testament always refers to the communication of information to others, except for Ps. xxii 18 and Job xxxviii 37, where it appears to have the meaning of the Qal, 'count'; but in both of these cases it could, and perhaps ought, to be pointed as Qal. In Job xxviii 27, however, no satisfactory meaning could be obtained by repointing the word as Qal, since the Qal yields no satisfactory sense.[3] We

---

[1] The two myths have certain similarities, and may be related to one another in some way. This is suggested by the fact, already noted, that xv 7*b* is almost identical with Prov. viii 25*b*, which refers to wisdom. The question is not material to the present argument.

[2] This is not true of Hos. ix 10, 'I saw your fathers in the wilderness'. Here רְאִיתִי is parallel with מְצָאתִי, and both verbs mean 'found' in the sense of 'came upon unexpectedly', the sense being metaphorical and therefore not seriously implying a lack of knowledge on the part of God.

[3] The normal meaning of the Qal is 'count, enumerate', and it requires a plural or collective object. Of the 27 occurrences, 23 are construed with numerals or plurals and 3 with collectives (בָּר, 'corn', Gen. xli 49; הָעָם, 'the people', 2 Sam. xxiv 10; 'Israel', 1 Chron. xxi 2). In all these cases the action of enumeration is involved, whether counting, counting out or measuring a quantity by repeated filling of a standard measure. In some cases

are therefore obliged to retain the pointing of the verb as Piel, and to conclude that it refers to the communication by God to others of the wisdom which he has seen.

הֵכִין has a wider variety of meanings, of which two may be relevant here. It frequently means 'to appoint' (to a task or function);[1] and in a number of passages[2] God's 'establishing' the world, mountains, sun and moon etc. is virtually equivalent to 'create'.[3]

חָקַר, when used with men as subject, means 'enquire, explore, examine, test, discover', always with the assumption of previous ignorance on the part of the subject; it is used in this way earlier in this chapter (verse 3) of men's underground exploration. With God as subject, however, it always[4] has as its object man, his heart or his secrets, and does not imply previous ignorance on the part of God. On the contrary, in every case it is used as a strong affirmation of the impossibility of hiding anything from God.[5] Thus in Job xxviii 27, with wisdom as object, it could be an affirmation that God had perfect knowledge of wisdom.

Each of these verbs can thus be made to yield a fairly

(especially Ps. lxxxvii 6) it is possible that the word means 'write down, record', but here also enumeration is involved, and in any case 'record' makes no good sense in Job xxviii 27. In the only case where the Qal is construed with a singular object (נֵדִי, Ps. lvi 9) the text is very doubtful, and some commentators (Duhm, Gunkel, Eaton) emend to a plural noun. The construction with צְעָדַי, 'my steps', as object in Job xiv 16; xxxi 4 has given rise to the supposition that it here has the sense of 'take note of, evaluate'; but the basic meaning in these two passages is still counting (of steps), and a plural object is still necessary. There is no Old Testament text in which סָפַר in the Qal unequivocally has a meaning which would give good sense in Job xxviii 27, where the object of the verb is singular.

[1] E.g. Josh. iv 4.
[2] Jer. x 12; xxxiii 2; Ps. lxv 7; lxxiv 16; Prov. viii 27.
[3] Some MSS have הֲבִינָה in place of הֲכִינָה; but this is probably an emendation. It is the easier reading.
[4] Jer. xvii 10; Ps. xliv 22; cxxxix 1; Job xiii 9.
[5] So Ps. xliv 22 'If we had forgotten the name of our God..., would not God discover (יַחֲקָר) this? For he knows (יָדַע) the secrets of the heart'; Job xiii 9 'Will it be well with you when he searches you out (יַחְקֹר)? Or can you deceive him, as one deceives man?'.

satisfactory meaning by itself; but the order in which they are arranged remains difficult to explain, whether they are considered as a consecutive series or as parallel pairs. Perhaps the most satisfactory rendering is as follows:

> Then he picked her out and made her known;
> he appointed her and understood her thoroughly.

The verse thus by no means necessarily implies the pre-existence of an uncreated wisdom who provided God with the knowledge needed to create the world, although it can be interpreted in this sense.[1] If it is so interpreted, it is curious that the Book of Job should contain references to two myths – those of wisdom and the *Urmensch* – which strongly resemble one another but seem hardly compatible. However, the chapter does at least make it clear that wisdom had some special relationship with God at the moment when he created the world. That God, having 'seen' her, then communicated this knowledge to others (which seems to be the only possible meaning of וַיְסַפְּרָהּ) also seems to imply the existence of an assembly of divine beings to whom God made a report, although nothing is said in this chapter which implies their active participation in the work of creation.

That wisdom should be one of the attributes of God especially emphasised in passages which refer to his creative activity is very natural, since חָכְמָה and תְּבוּנָה are the normal words for practical skill or craftsmanship.[2] They are used in this sense in a number of passages as attributes of God with no suggestion of personification.[3] In Prov. viii 22–31, where wisdom speaks of her origins, claiming to have been created before the world was made, and to have been present with Yahweh when he made it, there is a vivid personification of this divine attribute in which the author has attempted to

---

[1] Verse 23, which states that God 'knows the way to her', is equally ambiguous.
[2] E.g. they are both used of Bezalel, the maker of the furniture of the Tabernacle (Exod. xxxi 3; xxxv 31) and also of Hiram, the maker of the Temple furniture (1 Kings vii 14).
[3] Jer. x 12 = li 15; Ps. civ 24; cxxxvi 5; Prov. iii 19.

give greater vividness to his description by means of traits drawn from some female deity. I have argued elsewhere[1] that the figure of wisdom in this passage is, however, basically a personification of an attribute of Yahweh rather than a distinct being originally distinct from and uncreated by him, without whose assistance he could not have performed his acts of creation. If this interpretation is correct, Job xxviii remains the only passage in the Old Testament[2] in which there may be an *explicit* reference to wisdom as an independent supernatural being of this kind. In other words, the author of Job xxviii may have known a wisdom myth of which the author of Prov. viii was ignorant. But the uncertainties of the interpretation of this chapter, as also of the other passages in Job considered above, are too great for any conclusions to be drawn which could form the basis for the identification of the 'counsellor' of Isa. xl 13 f. with wisdom.

We refer next to the theory of de Boer[3] that Isa. xl 12–26 is 'a hymn to El (אֵל, verse 18), the High God, orderer of heaven and earth. He directed the spirit, "the motive power of the soul" of Jhwh, the god of Israel.' The point which de Boer is making is not entirely clear, for he goes on:

The very strength of El is delegated to Jhwh. Jhwh is the everlasting God, the Orderer of the whole earth; in verse 28, 'Have you not known? have you not heard?', the preacher asks his people. Therefore one may expect wonderful deeds. El is the counsellor with whom Jhwh took counsel, who instructed him and taught him the path of judgment, knowledge and the way of understanding (verses 13 f.).

De Boer here places a great deal of emphasis on the occurrence of the word 'El' in verse 18, whereas 'Yahweh' is used in verse 13. Yet elsewhere Deutero-Isaiah uses אֵל in passages where there can be no doubt that the word is

[1] *Wisdom in Proverbs* (SBT **45**), London, 1965, pp. 99–104.
[2] The later developments of the figure in Ecclesiasticus and the Wisdom of Solomon are outside the range of the present discussion.
[3] 'The Counsellor', p. 47.

nothing more than an appellation of Yahweh.[1] De Boer evidently has in mind the אֵל עֶלְיוֹן קֹנֵה שָׁמַיִם וָאָרֶץ of Gen. xiv 19, 22 and Eissfeldt's interpretation of Deut. xxxii 8 f. and Ps. lxxxii which makes Yahweh a member of the heavenly court attendant upon El Elyon.[2] In this case, however, he presumably cannot mean that Deutero-Isaiah himself held such a view: if he refers to it, it can only be in order to deny it. De Boer appears to be saying that Deutero-Isaiah's refutation takes the form of an assertion that El and Yahweh are identical: 'the very strength of El is delegated to Jhwh', so that if El was 'orderer of heaven and earth', so also is Yahweh. But if it was the intention of Deutero-Isaiah to put an end to a popular belief of this kind, his purpose would hardly be served by his using the kind of language which he uses in verses 13 f.: if El had 'instructed' Yahweh, he can hardly be identical with him! In short, the argument of de Boer that אֵל in verse 18 means a god called El who is identical with Yahweh's counsellor in verses 13 f. is extremely forced. Moreover, as has already been demonstrated, the scene depicted in these verses is one of Yahweh himself as king, presiding over a meeting of his council and receiving advice from a trained adviser whom he consults, rather than instructions from a superior.[3]

The Old Testament evidence, then, suggests that the image of the 'counsellor' in Isa. xl 13 f., though related to an Israelite belief in the existence of an assembly of divine beings over whom Yahweh presided like an earthly king and whom he sometimes consulted, is not derived from any corresponding Israelite belief in a specific office or function of counsellor. It might be argued that the image is based on the analogy of the human counsellor, familiar as a definite office

---

[1] xlii 5; xlv 15, 21. The same usage is found elsewhere in the Old Testament. See Eissfeldt, 'El and Yahweh'.

[2] Eissfeldt, art. cit. See pp. 44–6, above.

[3] Eissfeldt (art. cit., pp. 27 f.) includes Isa. xl 12 ff. among those passages where El is deliberately identified with Yahweh. He does not however suggest that the counsellor of verses 13 f. is intended to be El.

at the royal court. But if this were the case the absence of the idea from the earlier *religious* traditions of Israel would render the point a very weak one. The questions which Deutero-Isaiah is asking here have no point unless they are contrasting Yahweh's independence of a counsellor with some *known religious* tradition about a god who *does* need a counsellor. Such a tradition did not exist in Israel.

However, Israelite religious traditions were not the only ones with which Deutero-Isaiah and his fellow-exiles were familiar. The situation to which his prophecy was directed was one in which the Jewish exiles were subject to the influence of the Babylonian religion with which they were surrounded, and which they could not ignore.[1] It is therefore necessary to consider the possibility that the reference to the counsellor may be related to Babylonian mythology.

[1] For a recent study of the situation of the Jewish exiles see von Waldow, 'Anlaß und Hintergrund'.

CHAPTER X

THE DIVINE COUNSELLOR IN BABYLONIAN MYTH

The view that Deutero-Isaiah exercised his ministry in Babylonia among the Jewish exiles there rests mainly on the allusions in the book to the general political situation, in particular to the triumphant career of Cyrus king of Persia,[1] and to the situation of the community of Jews to whom the oracles are addressed. But it is also supported by a number of clear references in the book to Babylonian religious beliefs and practices, which suggest that the prophet and his Jewish audience had a more intimate acquaintance with Babylonian religion than would be probable unless they were themselves resident in Babylonia.

This fact has admittedly been somewhat obscured by the rather unconvincing attempts which have been made to go further and to prove that Deutero-Isaiah was not only familiar with Babylonian culture and religion, but was himself actually influenced by it to such an extent that he borrowed stylistic features and religious ideas from Babylonian literature and used them to express his own teaching. The literature of Mesopotamia has been ransacked in an attempt to find verbal and conceptual parallels to Deutero-Isaiah's language, style and teaching, and many such have been pointed out.[2] But in most cases the argument falls short of conclusive proof, and in some it is based on inadequate knowledge of the meaning of the texts. Apart from the question whether Deutero-Isaiah is likely to have been able

---

[1] See, e.g., S. Smith, *Isaiah Chapters XL–LV: Literary Criticism and History* (Schweich Lectures, 1940), London, 1944.

[2] Apart from the works mentioned below see, *inter alia*, F. Stummer, 'Einige Keilschriftliche Parallelen zu Jes. 40–66', *JBL* **45** (1926), pp. 171–89; J. W. Behr, *The Writings of Deutero-Isaiah and the Neo-Babylonian Royal Inscriptions*, Pretoria, 1937.

to read cuneiform and to have had an intimate knowledge of Babylonian literature, similarity of terminology and style is rarely sufficient to prove literary dependence unless there are other reasons to suspect it; and this is especially true in this case in view of the extent to which the Jew and Babylonian shared a common inherited cultural and linguistic background.[1] Attempts to show that Deutero-Isaiah not only knew, but adapted for his own use, specifically religious Babylonian phraseology and concepts are now therefore increasingly regarded with scepticism, especially by Assyriologists.

The precariousness of this approach to the Babylonian background of Deutero-Isaiah is well illustrated by the history of the interpretation of xlv 1. Here it is stated that Yahweh has grasped the right hand of Cyrus. It was long believed, and often repeated in the commentaries, that this is a metaphorical reference to a ceremony in which Marduk, symbolised by his statue, 'grasped' the right hand of the king of Babylon at the New Year Festival as a sign that he appointed, or reappointed, him king for the ensuing year. This theory was held to be confirmed by a passage in the Cyrus Cylinder in which Cyrus claims that Marduk had 'sought a just king, whose hand he might hold', and found him in Cyrus.[2] It is now known[3] that the phrase 'grasp the hand(s)' (*qāt* or *qātē ṣabātu*) is never used in the sense of 'appoint'. Of its possible meanings the one most appropriate to the context of the New Year Festival is 'lead, conduct', and the reference is to the king's conducting Marduk (not *vice versa*) from his temple Esagil to the Akitu house. The quite

[1] Cf. Labuschagne, *The Incomparability of Yahweh*, on biblical expressions asserting the incomparability of Yahweh. He concludes (pp. 124 ff.) that these, in spite of their similarity to expressions found in Babylonian literature, developed independently.

[2] So A. Jeremias, *The Old Testament in the Light of the Ancient East*, London, 1911, II, p. 274. The theory is reiterated in commentaries as recent as those of North (1964) and Westermann (ET 1969).

[3] See A. L. Oppenheim, *JAOS* **61** (1941), p. 270; the Chicago *Assyrian Dictionary*, vol. Ṣ, 1962, pp. 30–2. Cf. Oppenheim in *ANET*, p. 315.

different rite by which the king was confirmed in office had previously been performed in the Esagil, and was not witnessed by the public. The escorting of Marduk in procession to the Akitu house, which was witnessed by the public, was popularly regarded as the confirmation of the king's sovereignty, which explains why Cyrus set such store by it; but it did not correspond in any way to the statement in Isa. xlv 1.[1]

Nor does Engnell's theory[2] of the influence of Tammuz liturgies on the Servant Songs in Deutero-Isaiah provide evidence of Babylonian religious influence. Most scholarly opinion has judged the argument to be ill-founded; and even Engnell himself did not maintain that the influence was direct: he believed it to have been mediated at an earlier time to Israel through Canaan.

Babylonian influence has been more plausibly postulated with regard to one of Deutero-Isaiah's most characteristic stylistic features, the so-called 'hymn of self-praise' in which Yahweh speaks of his greatness and wonderful deeds in the first person.[3] Since the time of Gressmann[4] it has been recognised that these passages, which have no exact parallel elsewhere in the Old Testament, have their counterpart in Mesopotamian literature. A number of such hymns are now known in which the praise of a deity takes the form of a speech in the first person by the deity itself rather than, or in addition to, the usual address in the second person or statement in the third.[5] Most of this literature comes from a period much earlier than the neo-Babylonian, and is written in Sumerian, not Accadian; but there are a few examples of

---

[1] W. G. Lambert, in a private communication, expresses the opinion that Isa. xlv 1 cannot be connected with the Babylonian ritual in any way.

[2] I. Engnell, 'The 'Ebed Yahweh Songs and the Suffering Messiah in "Deutero-Isaiah"', *Bulletin of John Rylands Library* **31** (1948), pp. 54–93.

[3] Especially xliv 24–8; xlv 5–7; xlviii 12–13; l 2–3.

[4] 'Die literarische Analyse Deuterojesajas', pp. 285–94.

[5] H.-M. Dion, 'Le genre littéraire sumérien de l'"hymne à soi-même" et quelques passages du Deutéro-Isaïe', *RB* **74** (1967), pp. 215–34.

divine self-praise in Accadian from later periods, including two in which Marduk is the speaker.[1]

In spite of the undoubted similarity of style it is unlikely that there is more than coincidence here. Apart from general claims to omnipotence and incomparability there is no very close similarity of detail. Moreover it is intrinsically improbable that Deutero-Isaiah would deliberately have made use of such language which, if familiar to his audience, would be especially associated in their minds with pagan deities. Such a device would be more likely to give the impression that Yahweh was merely one among the gods than to emphasise his distinctiveness. It would tend to debase the coinage of Yahweh's claims to uniqueness and incomparability if the very language which Yahweh used about himself were the same as that used by Babylonian deities to make exclusive claims for themselves which, in a polytheistic religion, could hardly be taken literally even by their own worshippers.[2]

It has been suggested that, although Deutero-Isaiah is unlikely to have been familiar with these Babylonian hymns themselves, he may have known the formulae of self-praise from royal inscriptions which he could have seen displayed in public places, on which kings employed this style to praise themselves and their achievements.[3] This argument is

[1] They include a passage from an old Babylonian hymn to Ishtar (A. Falkenstein and W. von Soden, *Sumerische und akkadische Hymnen und Gebete*, Stuttgart, 1953, pp. 239 f., 381); a hymn in which the goddess Gula praises herself, from the Cassite period or later (W. G. Lambert, *Orientalia* **36** (1967), pp. 105–32); an incantation against demons in which Marduk is the speaker (W. G. Lambert, *Archiv für Orientforschung* **17** (1954–6), pp. 310–21; **19** (1959–60), pp. 114–19); and an autobiographical 'royal inscription' in which Marduk speaks about himself (H.-G. Güterbock, *ZA* **42** (NF **8**) (1934), pp. 79–84). Some of these texts are known to have been current in neo-Babylonian times and later. They appear to have been composed for various purposes.

[2] See Labuschagne, *The Incomparability of Yahweh*.

[3] Dion, 'Le genre littéraire sumérien de l'"hymne à soi-même"'. On the characteristics of these inscriptions see S. Mowinckel, 'Die vorderasiatischen Königs- und Fürsteninschriften. Eine stilistische Studie', *Eucharisterion* (Gunkel Festschrift), Part I, 1923, pp. 278–322.

5-2

extremely tenuous. Although royal inscriptions were publicly displayed in some periods there is no evidence for this practice in the Late Babylonian period; and the Late Babylonian inscriptions also differ from the earlier Assyrian ones in being generally pious rather than self-adulatory in tone. Moreover, it is extremely improbable that Deutero-Isaiah would have borrowed the bombastic language of human kings in setting forth the unique claims of Yahweh. It is more probable, therefore, that these passages are the result of Deutero-Isaiah's own combination of earlier Israelite formulae of the type 'I am Yahweh' with the style of the hymn or song of praise.[1]

These negative conclusions about the possibility of Deutero-Isaiah's dependence on literary texts do not, however, imply that he had no knowledge of Babylonian religion. The book abounds in evidence that the contrast between Yahweh and the Babylonian gods was constantly in his mind when he made his many statements about Yahweh's power and uniqueness. This contrast becomes explicit in the *Gerichtsrede* in which the gods and their worshippers are summoned to defend their claims to be effectively gods.[2] The descriptions of the manufacture of gods,[3] at least some of which are generally believed to come from Deutero-Isaiah's hand, seem to show a certain familiarity with the process.[4] The names of the two principal deities of Babylon at that time,

---

[1] See W. Zimmerli, 'Ich bin Jahwe', *Geschichte und Altes Testament* (Beiträge zur historischen Theologie **16**), Tübingen, 1953; the article was reprinted in Zimmerli, *Gottes Offenbarung. Gesammelte Aufsätze zum Alten Testament*, Munich, 1963.

[2] On the subject as a whole see H.-J. Boecker, *Redeformen des Rechtslebens im Alten Testament*, WMANT **14**, 1964. On the *Gerichtsrede* in Deutero-Isaiah see Gressmann, 'Die literarische Analyse Deuterojesajas', pp. 277–80; Köhler, *Deuterojesaja*, pp. 110–20; Begrich, *Studien zu Deuterojesaja*, pp. 18–41 (in *Theologische Bücherei* **20**, pp. 26–48); von Waldow, 'Anlaß und Hintergrund', pp. 37–46; Westermann, 'Sprache und Struktur', pp. 134–44.

[3] xl 19–20; xli 6–7; xliv 9–20; xlvi 6 f.

[4] Compare xl 19–20, with its mention of the various craftsmen who participate in the process, with a remarkably similar passage in the New Year Festival ritual, *ANET*, p. 331. This does not, of course, imply that Deutero-Isaiah was familiar with this text.

Bēl (one of the names of Marduk, used in the New Year Festival texts) and his son Nabû (Nebo) are mentioned in xlvi 1–2, where there may be an oblique reference to the festival procession. In xl 26 Yahweh's supremacy over the stars, which were believed by the Babylonians to control the destinies of men, is stressed, and the Babylonian belief in the efficacy of astrology and divination is made the subject of mockery in xlvii 12–13. xliii 10*b* ('Before me was no god formed, nor shall there be any after me') is an assertion that Yahweh is not involved in any theogony, and might be interpreted as a reference to the fact that Marduk and other Babylonian gods, having a genealogy, cannot make this claim, from which Deutero-Isaiah draws such important theological consequences. This may also be the implication of the phrase 'I (Yahweh) (am) the first and I am the last' (xliv 6; xlviii 12; cf. xli 4).

The fact that the Jewish exiles in Babylon had some knowledge of Babylonian religion, which is hardly surprising, does not in itself prove that they were familiar with the details of Babylonian mythology or with the functioning of the Babylonian pantheon, although even in the absence of direct evidence this would not be intrinsically improbable. The relatively large proportion of Deutero-Isaiah's prophecies which are devoted to arguments proving Yahweh's absolute superiority over the Babylonian gods and the latter's inability to do anything for their worshippers shows that among the exiles the temptation to apostatise was strong. This is what we should expect in the circumstances: residence for a whole generation in Babylonia, coupled with the sense of defeat which was theirs, and frustration with the falsehoods of their own prophets, whose predictions of a change in their fortunes had failed to materialise,[1] cannot have failed to produce apostates, and even those who hesitated will have been likely to acquire some knowledge of the local religion.

---

[1] Jer. xxix 8 f. On the situation in the exile see von Waldow, 'Anlaß und Hintergrund', pp. 124 ff.; 137 ff.; 156 ff.

Until recently a serious objection to the possibility of Deutero-Isaiah's having been familiar with Babylonian myths has been that these were believed to have been known only to a very restricted public. *Enuma Eliš*, for example, was recited by the priest alone in a *cella* before the statue of Marduk, and it was believed that it would have been unfamiliar to the ordinary Babylonian citizen. However, it has recently been convincingly argued that the use of myths was by no means restricted to the cult.[1] The contents of the two creation myths *Atra-ḫasīs* and *Enuma Eliš* show that this association with the cult is only a secondary one. In the case of *Atra-ḫasīs*, the author of the literary version has combined with a straightforward story of the creation of mankind a reference to a ritual practice connected with child-birth which patently does not belong to the context at all. Evidently the earlier versions of the myth were unconnected with this ritual; the author of the literary version has attempted to combine the two, presumably in order to provide the ritual, whose original significance had been forgotten, with a *raison d'être*.[2]

In the case of *Enuma Eliš* the discrepancy is between the character of the literary version itself and the ritual use to which we know from other sources that it was put. Although it is known to have been recited to the statue of the god Marduk in the course of the New Year Festival at Babylon at least from *c.* 700 B.C. and perhaps earlier...it must be observed that the epilogue to the epic states its purpose as being to educate mankind generally in the greatness of Marduk, with which the content wholly agrees. The cultic use does not seem to have been intended by the author.[3]

---

[1] W. G. Lambert, 'Myth and Ritual as Conceived by the Babylonians', *JSS* **13** (1968), pp. 104–12; W. G. Lambert and A. R. Millard, *Atra-ḫasīs: The Babylonian Story of the Flood*, Oxford, 1969, pp. 7 f. For 'myth and ritual' theories, see, *inter alia*, S. H. Hooke (ed.), *Myth, Ritual and Kingship*, Oxford, 1958; E. O. James, *Myth and Ritual in the Ancient Near East*, London, 1958; T. H. Gaster, *Thespis: Ritual, Myth and Drama in the Ancient Near East*, New York, 1961.

[2] Lambert, *art. cit.*

[3] Lambert and Millard, *Atra-ḫasīs*, p. 7.

Indeed, the contents of these myths suggest a quite different background. The most recent editors of *Atra-ḥasīs* remark that 'the content gives the impression of having been intended for public recitation..., and the Homeric poems offer a fair parallel... No doubt there was a class of illiterate story-tellers who had memorized their stock-in-trade.'[1]

This suggests that the story of such a myth (or epic) may have been known to a wide circle, and it is no longer necessary to suppose that Deutero-Isaiah's knowledge of Babylonian mythology implies an intimate knowledge of the rites of the New Year Festival. It is true that direct evidence concerning the dissemination of these stories among ordinary people is lacking; but it is clear that the purpose of *Enuma Eliš* as stated in the epilogue – the glorification of Marduk – cannot have been achieved simply through its cultic recital. The possibility of allusions to Babylonian mythology in Deutero-Isaiah is therefore not to be ruled out *a priori*.

Mesopotamian mythology recognised not only a society of the gods with both informal meetings and formal assemblies analogous to those of human society, but also a distinct office of counsellor in the divine society. There were, indeed, not one but many such counsellors. The most complete evidence for this is found in the so-called 'god lists'.[2] These lists were compiled, handed down, expanded and re-edited from Sumerian times to late Assyrian and Babylonian for a variety of reasons ranging from the collection of lexical information, as in the case of other types of word list, to the promotion of theological innovations. In some cases it is possible to trace the history of a list through a number of recensions and to observe the way in which the positions of various gods in the pantheon varied, and also the process of syncretism by which the more important deities absorbed lesser ones and took over their names.[3] The attributes of the various deities are also

---

[1] *Ibid.* pp. 7 f.

[2] See W. G. Lambert, 'Götterlisten', *Reallexikon der Assyriologie*, III, 473-9.

[3] See also Lambert, 'The Reign of Nebuchadnezzar I', pp. 4 f., 11-13, for a discussion of this and for a hymn to Marduk which also illustrates the process.

recorded. Some of these lists are known to have continued in use down to late Babylonian times.

The most comprehensive of these lists is a still unpublished one known as AN = *Anum*, a compilation of the Cassite period based on an earlier old Babylonian list. Here Marduk is given especial prominence, his fifty names being listed. The list contains about 1,970 names, and is systematically arranged. Each deity is first listed with all his names; then come the names of his spouse, the names of their children and, where appropriate, the names of the family and courtiers of the latter. Finally the names of the household servants of the father and mother are given. Each deity of any stature possessed his own divine court. Among its members there may be one or more deities with the title 'counsellor' (gu$_4$.dúb in Sumerian ideograms; *muntalku* in Accadian). Important deities such as Enlil and Marduk have two such counsellors.

Obviously the Jewish exiles will not have been familiar with such lists; but they may well have had some acquaintance with some of the mythological beliefs and traditions which the lists reflect. In particular, Deutero-Isaiah could well have known some version of one, or both, of the main Babylonian creation stories: *Atra-ḫasīs* and *Enuma Eliš*.[1] The former had long been the standard creation story; but at the time of Deutero-Isaiah it was in process of being replaced by *Enuma Eliš*, which had first come into prominence *c.* 700 B.C. or somewhat earlier, and by other myths of a similar character which emphasise the prominence of Marduk. Both myths give prominence to mutual consultation among the gods and to the formal divine council; and both refer to an office of counsellor of the gods.

In *Atra-ḫasīs* the creation of mankind and its subsequent

[1] For introduction, text, translation and commentary on *Atra-ḫasīs* see Lambert and Millard, *Atra-ḫasīs*. For translations of *Enuma Eliš* see A. Heidel, *The Babylonian Genesis*, 2nd edn, Chicago, 1951; *ANET*, pp. 60–72. A new edition of all the Babylonian creation myths is being prepared by W. G. Lambert.

fate are described. The work of creation is undertaken after a consultation between the principal deities, and is carried out jointly by Ea and the mother goddess. In this myth Enlil is frequently referred to as the counsellor (*māliku*) of the gods.

In *Enuma Eliš* the principal character is Marduk, who is hailed by the other gods as their king. Deliberations between the gods are particularly frequent in this poem, and occupy a considerable part of its total length: we may mention those between Apsu, Mummu and Tiamat (I 33 ff.), the more formal council of Tiamat and her associates (I 111 ff.), and the full assembly in which Marduk is elevated above the other gods (III 129–IV 32). Mummu, normally referred to as the 'vizier' (*sukkallu*) is in one place early in the narrative (I 66) called 'the counsellor' (*tamlāku*).

One of the most striking features of this poem is the role of Ea, the father of Marduk. In several respects his influence outweighs that of Marduk, in spite of the latter's frequently proclaimed kingship. It is Ea 'the all-wise' (I 60) who devises and executes the scheme for slaying Apsu, 'the begetter of the gods', and who renders powerless his adviser and vizier, Mummu; and it is he who begets Marduk. When Anshar, the president of the assembly, proposes that Marduk, as a young and vigorous god, should be chosen to avenge the gods against Tiamat, it is again Ea who gives advice to Marduk before the interview (II 96 ff.).

Ea is equally prominent in the account of creation. Most of the creative acts are attributed to Marduk alone (IV 137–46; v);[1] but the account of the creation of mankind presents a rather different picture.

According to Tablet VI, lines 1–16, Marduk conceives the idea of creating man and expounds it to Ea in the assembly. Ea approves of Marduk's intention, but proposes his own

[1] For a reconstruction and translation of Tablet v, missing in earlier editions, see B. Landsberger and J. V. Kinnier Wilson, 'The Fifth Tablet of *Enuma Eliš*', *JNES* **20** (1961), pp. 154–79.

method of going about it, which seems to be somewhat different from what Marduk has suggested.[1] Then in line 35 it is stated that 'Ea, the wise, created mankind'.[2] Line 38 appears to be an attempt to reconcile the discrepancy: 'as artfully planned by Marduk, did Nudimmud (i.e. Ea) create it'.

The confusion is due to the fact that the author of *Enuma Eliš* was attempting, without complete success, to put forward the claims of Marduk without flying completely in the face of the more ancient traditions such as are found in *Atra-ḥasīs*. He was not able completely to reconcile his theology with his material.[3] He introduced Marduk into his account of the creation of mankind by substituting him for the mother goddess; but he evidently felt unable to eliminate Ea, with the result that Ea and Marduk together have in effect become joint creators. It is only in the section proclaiming the names of Marduk (VI 122–VII 144) that it is unequivocally stated that Marduk alone created mankind (VII 29–32). But this section is known to be an independent document incorporated by the author of the poem.

Of the two types of creation story with which Deutero-Isaiah and his contemporaries might have been familiar, *Enuma Eliš*, with its glorification of Marduk, is the one which offers the most obvious possibilities of comparison with the Jewish traditions of creation. It is not confined, like *Atra-ḥasīs*, to an account of the creation of mankind, but deals with the creation of the world as well; and its purpose is the glorification of Marduk, whom it proclaims as undisputed king. If there was any Babylonian god who presented a challenge to Yahweh for the Jewish exiles, it was Marduk.[4]

---

[1] On this see S. G. F. Brandon, *Creation Legends of the Ancient Near East*, London, 1963, pp. 105 f.
[2] This is probably also true of line 33, where Lambert prefers the singular reading 'he created'.
[3] See Heidel, *The Babylonian Genesis*, p. 12; Brandon, *Creation Legends of the Ancient Near East*, pp. 105 f.
[4] Lambert, 'The Reign of Nebuchadnezzar I', p. 5, speaks of the supremacy of Marduk as 'verging on monotheism'.

At the same time *Enuma Eliš*[1] offered to Deutero-Isaiah more than one opportunity to show how Yahweh was superior to Marduk. The very birth of Marduk and the fact that he had not existed from the beginning but stood in a succession of generations of gods was sufficient for Jews (though not for Babylonians or other polytheists) to mark him as falling far short of true godhead as they understood it, and Deutero-Isaiah makes this point when Yahweh maintains that 'before me no god was formed, nor shall there be any after me' (xliii 10). But in Marduk's relation to his father Ea in *Enuma Eliš* there was a further opportunity to make an important debating point: both before and after his elevation as king, and even in the act of creation itself, Marduk did not act alone, but only on the advice of Ea, the wise god who had overcome Mummu, the former counsellor of the gods, and now stood in that relationship with regard to Marduk. Neither in planning nor in execution was the creation the sole work of Marduk.

This point could hardly have failed to make an impression on Deutero-Isaiah's audience. Apart possibly from the enigmatic Job xxviii discussed above,[2] the creation traditions of the Old Testament, though diverse, are all agreed on the essential belief that Yahweh and Yahweh alone created the world and mankind.[3] It was, indeed, one of the great achievements of Israelite religion that the polytheistic elements in the creation traditions which they had received had been purged at a very early date. In the 'J' story, which almost certainly dates from the early monarchy, the phrase 'the man has become like one of us' (Gen. iii 22) is, if it refers to the

---

[1] It is not suggested that Deutero-Isaiah knew the literary composition which goes by that name, but that he may have known some version of the same story. Traces of such other versions do in fact survive.

[2] Pp. 58–61 above.

[3] The view of R. A. Rosenberg ('Yahweh Becomes King', *JBL* **85** (1966), pp. 297–307) that Deutero-Isaiah's doctrine of Yahweh as the universal creator was derived from Assyrian beliefs concerning the moon-god Sin, revived in Babylonia by Nabonidus, completely ignores these Israelite traditions.

heavenly council, in itself an indication of the extent of the achievement, since the entire account, from its opening words 'In the day that Yahweh Elohim made the earth and the heavens' (ii 4*b*) contains not the slightest hint that any of these beings played any part at all in the acts of creation. The retention by 'P' of the phrase 'Let us make man in our image, after our likeness' (Gen. i 26), followed as it is in verse 27 by the singular form 'So God created' shows that the author was sufficiently sure of his readers' monotheism to allow the phrase, which he presumably found in his material, to stand. This is also shown by the fact that P is able to use the word 'God' (אלהים) in an unqualified way without danger of misunderstanding.

This insistence on the creation's being the unaided work of Yahweh alone is even more striking in the poetical traditions of the Old Testament, where Yahweh is represented as having first defeated the hostile sea or monsters such as Leviathan, Rahab or the *tannīnīm*.[1] It is questionable whether these mythological allusions were regarded as more than poetical figures: Deutero-Isaiah himself saw no objection to them.[2] In contrast to the positive role played by their counterparts in Babylonian and Ugaritic myths, where they constitute a real threat to their adversary, they appear in the Old Testament only in their defeat, and their only function is to serve as illustrations of Yahweh's invincible power. Thus although mythological language was permitted to remain in referring to the manner in which the creative acts were performed, nothing was allowed to obscure the uncompromising ascription of sole creative power to Yahweh. The heavenly beings around him can only observe, fear and praise him.[3]

The wisdom tradition represented by the Book of Job and Prov. iii 19 f.; viii 22–31 is in agreement with the others: in as far as 'wisdom' is associated with Yahweh in the creative acts it is only as one of his attributes.[4] The entire Old

[1] Ps. lxxiv 13–17; lxxxix 10–13.
[2] li 9.
[3] Ps. lxxxix 7–9.
[4] See pp. 58–61, above.

Testament evidence points to a consistent Israelite belief on this point; and Deutero-Isaiah reiterates it.

Since neither in the Canaanite tradition of the council of the gods nor in the Israelite traditions do we find any clear reference to a divine counsellor, it is reasonable to conclude that the questions in Isa. xl 13 f. are an intentional reference to a precise Babylonian mythological concept of a divine counsellor with which the Jewish exiles had become familiar, and that their intention was to point out the superiority of the claims of Yahweh, in this respect as in others, over those of Marduk.

CHAPTER XI

SUMMARY AND CONCLUSIONS

We may now summarise the evidence and draw some final conclusions about Deutero-Isaiah's theological and apologetic purpose.

It has been shown that the vocabulary used in Isa. xl 14 is that specifically pertaining to a royal council meeting. This suggests that Deutero-Isaiah was concerned here to raise the question of the nature of the divine realm in which ultimate decisions are made. This is in agreement with his insistence that Yahweh and Yahweh alone is the creator of the world,[1] that there is no god beside him,[2] and that he is 'the first and the last';[3] with his denial of theogony in xliii 10; and with his characterisation of the stars as the creatures (מִי־בָרָא אֵלֶּה) of the one and only Holy One (xl 26). The same strong emphasis is found in the frequent attacks on the gods: the identification of them with their images, their dismisssal as the invention of men, and the ridicule which is poured on them.

Therefore when in xl 13 f. we find a clear allusion to the idea of Yahweh as presiding over a council and taking advice from a counsellor, it is extremely probable that the council referred to is an assembly of heavenly beings. It is not a reference to the tradition which held that certain human beings were permitted on occasion to stand in Yahweh's סוֹד, since it is quite certain that these were called into the presence of God not to give advice but to hear his word and to receive his commands. Still less is it likely that there is a reference to some primeval man, a pre-existent *Urmensch*, who might have given advice to God at the time when the world was created, having snatched wisdom for himself. Such an interpretation of Job xv 7 f.; xxxviii 21 and similar passages is too tenuous

---

[1] xl 12, 22; xlii 5; xlv 18; xlviii 13.
[2] xliv 6, 8; xlv 5, 21; xlvi 9.   [3] xliv 6; cf. xli 4.

to deserve serious consideration. In other words, it cannot be established, nor is it probable, that there is any reference here to a *human* counsellor of God.

It is equally improbable that there is no precise reference at all in these verses: that the 'Who?' of the rhetorical questions has no specific person in mind but is no more than a rhetorical device to express in a more lively manner a thought which could have been expressed equally clearly by a negative statement that 'no-one has ever comprehended the mind of Yahweh' etc. The vocabulary employed is too precise for this to be the case: the reader cannot do otherwise than to think of Yahweh and his heavenly court; and the אִישׁ עֲצָה must refer to some supernatural being, real or hypothetical.

Of the three main types of possible interpretation of the אִישׁ עֲצָה as a supernatural being, the least probable is that it refers to wisdom. In Job xxviii there is a reference to some mysterious association between God and wisdom at the time when the world was created, and Prov. viii 22–31 also depicts wisdom as present at the creation. But as we have seen, there is insufficient evidence to demonstrate that there existed in Old Testament times a tradition which saw wisdom as a fully fledged personality capable of acting as Yahweh's adviser and teacher.

There remain therefore two possible sources of the allusion: the Israelite tradition of the heavenly council and the Babylonian pantheon as it was conceived in the time of Deutero-Isaiah.

As we have seen, the concept in Israelite tradition seems to have been a very fluid one. There is no consistency of nomenclature: in 1 Kings xxii 19–22 we have the 'host of heaven' with 'a spirit' acting as adviser; in Isa. vi only the seraphim are mentioned, and presumably it is they with whom Yahweh consults; in Job i–ii the assembly consists of the בְּנֵי אֱלֹהִים, among whom is the Satan. There are other variations. The concept itself is clear enough, but, apart from

6-2

the post-exilic passages, in which Satan plays a role similar in some respects to that of counsellor, there is no clear evidence of an office of אִישׁ עֵצָה distinct from ordinary membership of the council. In I Kings xxii, for example, we are told that 'one said one thing, and another said another'. But the picture of such discussions of policy at Yahweh's court was evidently familiar to pre-exilic Israelites, and it is difficult to believe that this was entirely absent from the mind of Deutero-Isaiah when he wrote these verses.[1]

However, the Babylonian pantheon, as we have seen, offers more precise parallels. Since we do not know which of the Babylonian myths were familiar to the Jewish exiles or in what version, we cannot be sure whether Deutero-Isaiah is referring in xl 13 f. to the Babylonian concept of the divine counsellor in general or to some particular figure or figures. The function of Ea in *Enuma Eliš* makes him a likely candidate, but some other deity may be intended – perhaps even Nabû, the scribal god credited with universal wisdom, who took a prominent part in the New Year Festival procession at Babylon, and who evidently made an impression on Deutero-Isaiah, since he is the only Babylonian god apart from Marduk mentioned by name in the book, and mentioned in close association with Marduk (xlvi 1). But more important than the precise identification of the deity alluded to are the facts that the Babylonian myths attach much greater importance to the advice given than does the Israelite tradition, and that unlike the Israelite tradition as far as it is known to us they assert that such advice was offered and accepted on the occasion of the creation of the world, to which Deutero-Isaiah is referring here.

It is therefore extremely probable that in these verses Deutero-Isaiah, though having in mind the Israelite tradition

---

[1] For the view that Deutero-Isaiah not only knew, but himself believed in the concept of the heavenly council of Yahweh, see pp. 82–4 below. In the present study it has seemed preferable to work out the interpretation of xl 13 f. without reference to the passages cited in Cross' article, which would have introduced a further complication.

of the heavenly council, was referring to the Babylonian mythology of his time. His polemic is not against the traditional Israelite concept, nor against any innovations which may have been introduced into it as a result of Assyrian or Babylonian influence during the later monarchy. The Jewish exiles had not carried with them from their home any belief in a pantheon with Yahweh at its head. It was rather after their arrival in Babylonia that they had encountered a full polytheistic system which challenged the traditional Israelite conception of God. The prophecies are addressed not to those who had altogether abandoned their faith in Yahweh but to those who were attracted by the plausible idea that as in human affairs, so in divine, two heads (or more) were better than one when it came to making important decisions, and that the world was both created and ruled by committee rather than by the fiat of a single supreme deity. It is not clear to us how Yahweh may have been thought to fit into the Babylonian polytheistic scheme. But it may be that there were those among the exiles who, while accepting Yahweh as the supreme god, were inclined to understand this concept in Babylonian terms by transforming the hitherto innocuous concept of the heavenly council into something like a pantheon in which that supremacy was in fact a limited one.

This would account for the statement in xl 26 that the stars and heavenly bodies whom Yahweh 'brings out by number and calls by name' are not, as in the Babylonian system, in which this function is performed by Marduk,[1] gods such as Anu, Enlil and Ea, but simply Yahweh's creatures – a point very similar to that made by Deutero-Isaiah's near contemporary, the author of the Priestly creation story (Gen. i 14–18). It is into this context of thought that we must fit xl 13 f., a passage which recalls the earlier Israelite tradition as against the Babylonian, and asserts by implication that the idea of a counsellor god, in the sense of one without whose counsel Yahweh could not have created

---

[1] *Enuma Eliš* iv 141–v 44.

the world, is unthinkable for believers in Yahweh: Yahweh is God in an absolute sense unknown to the Babylonians.

This interpretation enables us to understand better what is frequently referred to as Deutero-Isaiah's 'doctrine of monotheism'. It has recently been convincingly argued that side by side with his uncompromising monotheism there are clear indications that he retained a belief in the Israelite concept of Yahweh's heavenly council.[1] The main passage in question is xl 1–8.[2] The plural imperatives ('Comfort, comfort my people' etc.) with which in verse 1 Yahweh begins his instructions, suggest a scene in which Yahweh addresses his angelic heralds, and this impression is confirmed by the unexplained voices (קוֹל) in verses 3 and 6, which give instructions (again in the plural: to other angelic beings?) for the preparation of the highway and instruct the prophet what message he is to proclaim: these appear to be the voices of the heralds carrying out their instructions. It is unlikely that these forms of speech are simply poetical images, or that the prophet was unconscious of having employed them.

There is a certain resemblance here to Isa. vi, although the setting is not described, and the existence of the heavenly beings is only hinted at. It should be noted that there is no suggestion of Yahweh's asking for or accepting advice: the concept of the heavenly council has reached its final stage of development, and is now no more than a means by which the supreme God instructs his heavenly servants. Their sole function is to obey, and they are to all intents and purposes the angels of later Jewish literature.

[1] Especially F. M. Cross, 'The Council of Yahweh in Second Isaiah', *JNES* **12** (1953), pp. 274–8, followed by Brown, 'The Pre-Christian Semitic Concept of "Mystery"', p. 420; Cooke, 'The Sons of (the) God(s)', pp. 42–4; Albright, *Yahweh and the Gods of Canaan*, p. 167; McKenzie *et al.* The idea had already been suggested by Robinson, 'The Council of Yahweh', p. 155, and Wright, *The Old Testament against its Environment*, p. 37 n. 52. None of these authors refers to xl 13 f.
[2] Cross suggests that the concept is also alluded to in xliv 26; xlviii 20 f.; lii 7–10, but his arguments here are less convincing.

Deutero-Isaiah is a most consistent prophet, and we should be wrong to find inconsistency here. The explanation is to be sought rather, as various writers have suggested,[1] in the Israelite concept of personality. The idea of God as an isolated monad would have been wholly incomprehensible both to the prophet and to his audience. Just as the human personality was inconceivable except in the context of a society, so also was the divine. The concept of Yahweh as possessed of unlimited power, far from leaving him in isolation, actually required as its corollary that, like any human king, he would have at his command a body of servants and messengers attending upon him to carry out his commands. The use of the term 'monotheism' to describe Deutero-Isaiah's teaching has tended to obscure this, and quite wrongly to isolate him from his historical context in the history of Israelite religion as if he were an entirely unique phenomenon, a Greek philosopher born before his time. There is no evidence for this view. He was concerned rather to preserve the traditional Israelite view of God than to introduce novel doctrines. The danger which he saw it as his task to combat was a twofold one: the tendency of the exiles to regard the Babylonian gods rather than Yahweh as the rulers of the world, and their inclination to regard Yahweh as similar in nature to the Babylonian gods. He countered the first by adducing arguments to prove that the Babylonian gods were powerless and even non-existent; he argued against the second by referring scornfully – as in xl 13 f. – to the inherent weakness of a creator god who did not possess by himself sufficient wisdom or power to carry out his task, in contrast with the Israelite tradition.

There is therefore no inconsistency in the fact that, although Deutero-Isaiah strenuously denied the existence of

---

[1] Especially A. R. Johnson, *The One and the Many in the Israelite Conception of God*, Cardiff, 2nd edn 1961; Robinson, 'The Council of Yahweh', p. 156; *Inspiration and Revelation*, pp. 169 f.; Wright, *The Old Testament against its Environment*, p. 36; T. C. Vriezen, *The Religion of Ancient Israel*, London, 1967, p. 36.

other gods and set no limit to the might of Yahweh, he retained, and passed down to succeeding generations, the concept of a heavenly court. If he introduced any innovation into this concept, it was that he made it even clearer than any before him that the function of its members was not to assist Yahweh in making his decisions but simply to carry out his commands.

INDEX OF BIBLICAL REFERENCES

INDEX OF AUTHORS CITED

INDEX OF AUTHORS CITED

ÉCHÉANCE DATE DUE

Please return to the University of Sudbury
Prière de remettre à l'Université de Sudbury